ALL THE WAY

ALL THE WAY

MY LIFE IN FOUR QUARTERS

JOE NAMATH

with Sean Mortimer and Don Yaeger

Little, Brown and Company

New York Boston London

Little, Brown and Company
Hachette Book Group
1290 Avenue of the Americas, New York, NY 10104
littlebrown.com

First Edition: May 2019

Little, Brown and Company is a division of Hachette Book Group, Inc. The Little, Brown name and logo are trademarks of Hachette Book Group, Inc.

The publisher is not responsible for websites (or their content) that are not owned by the publisher.

The Hachette Speakers Bureau provides a wide range of authors for speaking events. To find out more, go to hachettespeakersbureau.com or call (866) 376-6591.

Image credits: page 1, photograph by Bill Meurer / NY Daily News Archive via Getty images; page 7, courtesy of Beaver County Genealogy and History Center; page 129, photograph by James Drake / Sports Illustrated / Getty Images; page 155, photograph by Walter Iooss Jr. / Sports Illustrated / Getty Images; page 189, photograph by Bob Peterson / The LIFE Images Collection / Getty Images; page 215, photograph © Jessica Namath. All additional images, unless otherwise noted, are from the author's private collection.

ISBN 978-0-316-42110-2 (regular edition) / 978-0-316-53022-4 (exclusive edition) / 978-0-316-42537-7 (large-print edition) / 978-0-316-49011-5 (signed edition) / 978-0-316-49010-8 (BN.com signed edition)
LCCN 2018955558

10 9 8 7 6 5 4 3 2 1

LSC-C

Printed in the United States of America

*To the underdogs and the favorites:
It isn't how we get knocked down that
matters, it's how we get back up.*

CONTENTS

THE WARM-UP

I finished voluntarily reading my first book when I was in my early twenties. Growing up, our family didn't emphasize education much and definitely didn't have books lying around the house. We just weren't the kind of family to sit down and read. The paper only got a peek from me because it had the sports section. But, now, all these years later, my daughters, Jessica and Olivia, have the things stacked up around the house, and my granddaughter Jemma reads through those Harry Potter books like they're magazines.

I, too, have grown to love reading, but that took until the age of twenty-two to plant the first seed. I was at LaGuardia airport getting ready to leave for an away game and picked up a copy of a book about the Boston Strangler. An alarming set of eyes stared out at me from the cover and instantly grabbed my attention.

After finishing that book, and still to this day, I've always stayed alert in case a loose horse comes into play. And it certainly helped me establish my hotel room routine. The first thing I do is find my floor's emergency exits.

Then I scope out the shadowy areas in my room where someone might be hiding—I check under the bed, behind the curtains, shower, and closets. Only after knowing I'm alone will I take off my coat, unpack, and really settle in. Call it my suspicious Gemini side, but I know my vivid imagination has helped keep me on my toes all these years. I can even remember a time back in 1951, when I was eight, going to see *The Thing from Another World* at a Beaver Falls theater with my buddies Linwood and Freddie. Maaan, I was so scared I ran for the exit but stopped just short of the doors. My brave Gemini side decided I could *safely* peek around the wall from the back of the theater and still have a quick escape route in case that creature jumped out of the screen.

I still have fear run through my bones from time to time. Heck, just the thought of writing another book intimidated me. But that's the thing about fear, it can cripple you or it can motivate you to overcome the fear itself. And an urge to triumph over adversity and challenges has always been part of my personality. So if you're reading my book you know I've managed to overcome this literary challenge.

At first, writing down my life, A–Z, from the beginning to now, seemed to make the most sense. But before I knew it, I basically had a bad book report on myself. Finding the right approach had been a real struggle until my daughter Jessica asked me what I wanted to accomplish. Sometimes blunt simplicity is a powerful tool to dig out what you need. Well, I found myself answering: I'd like to share good times, tough moments, and bad experiences. Hopefully you'll find your own inspiration from my journey through this life that I've been lucky enough to survive. So far, at least. And if these pages can accomplish that, then they'll be well worth my effort to find the words to fill them.

* * *

There was notoriety around my life—and some of it was true. Sure, I did enjoy the company of a lot of lovely ladies. I wore fur coats on the sidelines and a Fu Manchu when I felt like it. But writing this book helped me feel even more connected and grateful to those who have played a part in my life, even the folks who come up to me on the street and give a greeting or shake my hand—those strangers who we make connections with to feel part of a larger purpose.

There's a news clip of me being interviewed after winning the Super Bowl, and I'm sitting there, shirtless and sweaty, with black grease under my eyes.

"Joe, you're king of the hill," my buddy Sal Marchiano says.

"No," I said. "*We're* king of the hill. We got the team, brother."

I might have been referring to my brothers on the Jets right then, but now I know that all those people we interact with while on life's journey make up the team.

Because what if we really were alone and didn't have each other to share the good and get through the bad? We have to learn from each other's shortcomings and triumphs. Because change, man, that's a constant and a certainty that is always presenting us with two simple choices: We either change in a positive fashion and get better, or change for the worse and regress.

You see, and this might be oversimplifying, but one of my goals here is to show you how I've changed, both positively and negatively, through the course of life. I also hope to communicate this evolution like I've been taught to communicate while calling a play in the huddle. Because when I'm talking to teammates, I need to say it clearly and with confidence. If a player has any doubts when he breaks the huddle, odds are that the play is not going to work.

How the heck did we start with the Boston Strangler and get talking about the positive power of connections and huddle etiquette?

That's life, man, all the way.

CHAPTER ONE

Something isn't right. My chest is tight, and I'm just distracted, man, distracted. I'm drinking my daily eight-ounce Cheribundi at the kitchen table as an afternoon storm starts rolling in, slowly darkening our summer sky. Nothing out of the ordinary for August in south Florida, but I'm sure outta my element. I decide to pull up the definition of "memoir" on my iPad: "A record of events written by a person having intimate knowledge of them and based on personal observation." Boy, that just isn't me. I don't have a lot of practice talking about myself unless I'm answering questions. Growing up with three older brothers, somebody else was always talking, louder than I ever could. It just feels negative, man. Negative.

I'm into that Gemini astrology stuff, you know? We're versatile, able to adapt to situations just as easily as we can (hopefully) find our way out of them. So the idea of having my life drawn out, step by step, makes me uncomfortable. Has me feeling boxed in. But thinking out of the box is what got me into this mess. Am I sharing things that I don't really need to share? My mind always checks itself, always asks questions. Always weighs the "What if?" Checking alternatives is just part of who I am. In elementary school I didn't ask questions, like a dope. There was a side of me embarrassed to let on that I didn't know the answer. Now, I just keep searching or ask for help until I feel satisfied with the answer. To say "I don't know" is not embarrassing any- more. I don't like not knowing, and when something makes me aware of my limitations, I try to go beyond and find the answer. And, man, is there a lot out there that I don't know.

As I thought about different approaches to the book, though, family members and friends had offered sugges- tion after suggestion. I tried the obvious, like starting from my birth on May 31, 1943, in Beaver Falls, Pennsylvania, and then going into a childhood with siblings spread out in front of me. John, who we all called Sonny, because Dad called him son, was twelve years older; Bob came in at nine my senior; and Frank and Rita only had six years on me. We adopted my sister, Rita, when I was four, so Mom finally got a daughter and all us boys landed ourselves a sister.

The day Rita arrived, I was peeking from behind a wall outside of the front room, too shy to introduce myself but unable to stop staring. A quiet girl with long dark pigtails down to her waist, she wore a straw boat hat and "car coat," which came to about mid-thigh. Much later, I heard rumors that she may have been my father's daughter with another woman, but I didn't know or care enough to investigate any further. And if that was the case, then my mom was raised to a level of sainthood in my eyes because she immediately seemed to love my sister unconditionally. We all did. She fit in so naturally it felt like she'd known us forever. Or however long forever could feel to a four-year-old. In due time though, I could annoy her just as well as I could my older brothers. And vice versa.

* * *

Starting at the beginning doesn't seem like such a bad way to begin, I suppose. After all, Beaver Falls was and is a beautiful small town, something Norman Rockwell would have painted, with rolling hills, rambling creeks, and railroad tracks. A few mills manufacturing pipes, steel tubing, glass, and enamel speckle the background, adding grit to the landscape. That's not a dig, of course. My dad worked at one for decades, and our town seemed less affected by much of the ugliness and turmoil that other parts of the country struggled with at the time.

Dad stayed in decent shape with his millwork and often took me to the bowling alleys for his league games. Hanging out with him one-on-one was the best. I'd watch some of the games with my dad, all gussied up in his fancy team bowling shirt sponsored—and paid for—by some furniture store or local gas station. But sponsor or not, dress or casual clothes, Dad was always neat and clean.

The older kids, just out of high school, hung out at the pool halls, and I'd see them playing through the haze of smoke at the back room of Woolworth's bowling alleys. You'd sometimes hear rough talk and racial slurs in the poolrooms, but schools weren't segregated, and friends came in all colors, and if there was a dividing line, it wasn't boldly drawn. I'm not so sure it ever is on the side of the tracks I come from. Lower End neighborhoods were filled with ethnic mixtures of other steel plant workers.

Mom and Dad bought a corner house on Sixth Street

and Eighth Avenue with a potholed dirt road on the side, often sprayed with oil to keep the dust down. Sixth Street was laid with cobblestone and you could hear the horses pulling wagons of fresh vegetables and fruit a block away. My grandparents emigrated from Hungary, so my parents fit right into a neighborhood filled with Italians, Hasidic Jews, blacks, Greeks, Polish, Irish, and whoever or whatever. On the Lower End we all just mixed it up and the only designation with us kids was how well somebody hit the ball or who ran the fastest.

* * *

So my biggest issue with the chronological timeline format is simply that my memory doesn't work like that. There are ebbs and flows, with some moments expanding into great big bursts of joy affecting so much of my life, while other times, entire years even, seem to skip by. Being locked into one certain way, having only one option in a given situation— that's always something I try to avoid. To this day in football, the best play is the run-pass option, because you have flexibility to go with more than one choice. Knowing my choices and calling plays from the read and feel I was given on the field is something I'd loved since high school. When I first started playing pro ball for the Jets, our head coach, Weeb Ewbank, would walk up to me on the sidelines and ask what I liked, meaning what play I'd call when I got back on the field.

"How can I know?" I'd say. "I'm not out on the field with the ball." I didn't have enough pertinent information to know what I'd like to run, play-wise. I didn't know how much time would be left on the clock, where we'd get possession, how the defense would set up. Things that quarterbacks today aren't even bothered with. I'm amazed at the efficiency of the game and how it's evolved because looking back, it's certainly far less sophisticated.

Sometimes in a huddle, I wouldn't have a feel for a play so I'd ask, "Anybody got anything?" The guys knew that meant that I was asking them for input—a particular play they'd like to run. Other times they'd let me know if someone kept lining up on their outside or inside shoulder and they could get an angle block on a particular play. Or outside receivers would mention they could run a route on a cornerback, knew they had someone beat. I liked including my teammates and I think they liked being included. So if they had something, we'd run it. If they didn't, then I'd just give a formation and call a "check with me." That meant I'd let 'em know what play we'd run when we got on the line of scrimmage. The key was to see how the other team set up against our offensive formation. I'd notice small, specific things the defense would give me, maybe see who was limping, or a certain detail I'd picked up from watching film the week before, and my decision would be made. I'd call the best play for the defensive look they gave us.

A great example was a strong safety for the Boston Patriots my rookie year who would stagger his feet differently when rotating deep outside or inside as opposed to playing man or zone under. He was a nice guy, though, so after a game we were at a bar together and I mentioned it to him. I shouldn't have, since we played each other again, and that was the only time I did that, but I liked him. And I knew I'd find another nuance that would trigger me to call an audible; some play that'd let Maynard find a hole to settle in or let Snell punch through the line with the ground game. I'd wait and keep my options open.

* * *

So I had meetings with the book people and talked to my longtime friend and advisor Jimmy Walsh and my daughters, all the while fishing around for something that felt right. At one point or another, they all mentioned the 1968 World Championship. I know, it's Super Bowl III, but back then I can't remember anyone calling it that. Not that what the game was branded mattered much. What's important were the stakes. This was a tale of two leagues: the best of the straitlaced and respectable National Football League, established with a solid sense of history and respectability, against the best of the scrappy American Football League, generally considered subpar and peppered with misfits and rejects who were cut from the NFL.

I'd only ever watched that game from start to finish once before, and that was at the beginning of the 1969 season with the rest of our team at training camp. Maybe not even the whole game then. You see, the offensive team watched the offensive clips and the defensive team, of course, watched the defensive clips. Forget iPads and smart phones, we didn't even have videocassette recorders back then. To see a game that wasn't on television, the Jets had to get ahold of an actual film copy of the game and thread the reels on a projector.

In fact, the Jets furnished each quarterback and defensive play caller with a film projector for our homes. I'd walk out of practice with three or four reels under my arms. I studied those films hard, too. Certainly with more enthusiasm than any other type of studying in my life. Most early evenings, I'd set up the projector, thread the film, get my notebook and pen—and pour myself a Scotch on the rocks. I either watched from my couch or set it up so the film projected on a wall I could see from the kitchen. I always kept a notepad, too, while reviewing the next opponent's tendencies in case there was something I wanted to share with the appropriate people. I'd watch a play, rewind it, make notes on foot placement and what defense they played on, say, first-and-10. I'd visualize a lot so when I was on the field I'd be able to recognize what they were doing before the snap: I'd *anticipate* if they were gonna play man, zone, or zone–man under—one of the toughest defenses to read. By the time we were given reels most weeks, the coaches would have already broken the film down, given us the plays we were going to use, and told us what to expect given down and distance. I never had a set amount of time that I studied. I'd just keep going until that gnawing feeling of not knowing enough, not being prepared for all imaginable situations, faded. Then, well, I'd be finished with my homework, and that meant it was time to go out and play.

Nowadays you just swipe the screen to get a video, and Scotch is no longer necessary to relax me. So I got to thinking, why not watch the game film for old times' sake and see if gets my creative juices flowing. There are certainly times when somebody asks me a question about the game, about a certain play, and man, it just pops me back onto that field. But I wonder if I remember it the way you saw it?

The NFL posted the entire NBC broadcast online in anticipation of the fiftieth anniversary, so as the late-afternoon thunder rumbles, I pull the link up and turn the volume off, something I've always done so I'm able to focus on the game without the play-by-play distraction.

The old NBC logo zooms onto my screen. NBC SPORTS PRESENTS THE AFL/NFL CHAMPIONSHIP GAME—THE SUPER BOWL. Huh, I guess they really did call it the Super Bowl. I watch as the camera pans over Miami's Orange Bowl field, scanning the marching band. Seeing the field again gets the memories going and feelings start to flow.

CHAPTER TWO

The game started at three p.m. on Sunday, January 12th. But already my head is back to hours before that, in Fort Lauderdale, as the New York Jets walked out of the Galt Ocean Mile Hotel and into the thick Florida air. Why had we stayed at the Galt? Because Coach Vince Lombardi and the NFL's Green Bay Packers had booked it the year before and won the World Championship by beating the AFL's Oakland Raiders. Coach Ewbank had picked the hotel, and Frank Ramos, the Jets media director, told me, "Weeb figured if it was good enough for Vince Lombardi and his victorious Packers, it was good enough for us." And it was terrific. I didn't know where our opponents were staying— nor did I care—but it wasn't the Galt.

Watching the commentators talk silently, I begin remembering things I thought about that morning, like hoping the skies would clear. Rain obviously makes stuff slippery and I've yet to meet a quarterback who prefers throwing a wet football. I had big enough hands, but a wet ball and wet hands can lead to some slippage and sloppy throws, a problem I once tried to solve by getting Hamp, our equipment manager, to clip the points off five thumbtacks. By the time he was finished they were down to maybe one-sixteenth of an inch. We then got tape and fastened them onto the tips of my fingers and thumb—sharp side out, slightly sticking through the tape. It was a rainy, muddy game day at Shea Stadium against the Denver Broncos and when I went out onto the field and started warming up, throwing short tosses, the ball stuck to the tacks just long enough so the release was too low. My passes were going right into the ground.

And we were screwing up the balls. After half a dozen or so bad passes, the pigskin was torn up. So the tacks didn't work, but hey, in the days before playing gloves, the idea was worth a try. And blaming rain for a bad throw simply wasn't an option. Nobody wants to hear excuses, even a legitimate one. Just ask my brothers.

Bob and Frank were the ones who taught me how to throw a football from the ear to get a quick release. That makes a difference of split seconds. Bob played quarterback until he quit high school, so he played the position the best. I've gotta believe Frank developed his throwing style from studying Bob, too. I'd noticed how Frank as a catcher would throw the baseball without a long windup motion. And the fact that I was still small for my age didn't stop him from throwing it with a lot of heat when we played catch. Growing up with rough, all-American brothers, they were going to teach me things, sure, but in a rough, demanding, *do it now and how I tell you* style. They could have just showed me once and left it at that, but they wanted me to do it perfectly.

And I loved tossing the ball around! I was a baseball fan, especially of Pittsburgh Pirates right fielder Roberto Clemente. I'd mimic the way he caught fly balls and even bobbed my head like he did when he got into the batter's box. We lived about thirty miles from Pittsburgh, and my uncle Joe and my older brother Bob used to take me to Pirates games.

I remember one specific night game with Bob—the Pirates were behind by three or four runs so Bob made us leave. We were driving out of Pittsburgh, listening to the game on the radio, and the Pirates started coming back. I'll be damned if they didn't end up winning. Even Bob was angry at himself.

But I still got to see Roberto, the first player whose style spoke to me. While he was an athlete, there was something else about the way that he, and only he, threw and caught the baseball. He carried himself like royalty on the field. Maybe it was the combination of his swagger and seeing how my older brothers dressed that got me blending sports with fashion in my head. And then, when the varsity baseball team sat for our photo, I was in the front row along with the other seniors. I always wore sunglasses in the outfield and called them "cheaters." I liked the way they looked so I'd figured, what the heck—I might as well wear them when I wasn't playing. It wasn't anything specific and I wasn't trying to be disrespectful—there was no "look" I was going for. But it isn't the glasses that I focus on when seeing that photo today. For me, what pops are the shoelaces. I had specifically taken them out of my high-top Converse that I used for basketball and added them to my baseball shoes. I distinctly remember the white laces popping against the black shoes.

Unlike most parents back then, Dad was always involved with my athletic activities, but the family situation had gotten complicated long before that varsity baseball picture was taken. My parents divorced when I was in the seventh grade. Frank and Rita had graduated and moved out, and I was living alone in an apartment with Mom above a tavern called Club 23.

I still had a good relationship with my dad. Most Christmases, if not every one, I'd meet him at the CIO Union Hall, Local 1082, where the kids would each receive a brown paper bag with an orange, an apple, a candy cane or some hard candy. He was also there at games and even some practices, observing the goings-on.

I know this because I must have been fourteen, playing in some Pony League game—the sort that some of the dads helped shuttle us to—when a teammate made an error and my dad yelled at him as he was coming off the field after the inning. He was off to my right in the dugout, and the tone of voice that Dad used made me react. My teammates looked away, embarrassed, clearly hurt, and it made me protective. We never yelled at one another when we messed up—we all committed errors. So I turned around and in a harsh tone said, "Dad, don't do that. Don't yell at him."

I didn't know what I was expecting, but my dad transformed, snapping his head toward me. His eyes lit up and he said, "Shut up," and he raised his hand like he was going to give me a slap.

I instinctively put my hands up, bracing for a blow that never came. We looked into each other's eyes and he turned and walked away.

After that, we did not talk to each other for two years or so until I was in high school.

When we eventually saw each other again, we spoke about what had happened in the dugout that day. It wasn't complicated. He was angry that I had challenged him. I was mad that he came down on my teammate. Finally, he got to the heart of the matter.

"Son, you raised your hands to me."

I didn't know what he was talking about at first. Had to think back to the situation. Then I remembered that I really did put my hands up, but those open hands must have meant one thing to me and another to him. Dad, it turns out, thought I wanted to fight him. When I explained I was being defensive, protecting myself because I thought he was about to hit me, we both agreed to put the moment behind us and learn from it.

And we did. Because otherwise, most of the memories around my baseball-playing days are the kind I hope I never forget. In fact, my senior year, we won the WPIAL—the Western Pennsylvania Interscholastic Athletic League—championship. I realize that might not be the World Series, but baseball was a serious sport in western Pennsylvania, and being high school champions was an achievement that we were all proud of. I have always had two goals in sports: the first is to make the team and the second is to win the championship. I wanted to be a champion—that was the ultimate goal.

But when in that batter's box, or fielding and throwing from the outfield, I knew I had a lot of room for improvement. I wasn't fooling myself, man. Sports were taken very seriously in my area—they were a way to get into college and a better life. Dads often said, "Son, you're going to get a uniform when you get out of school. It might be an army, navy, or marine one, or a baseball, football, or basketball one—it's up to you." So getting noticed always gave me a little dose of self-confidence, the variety that can't help but make you move on up at whatever else it is you're doing in life. Sports provided future opportunities as well as confidence.

I gotta tell ya, though, I was surprised. And truly thankful for all the attention I was getting as a high school kid from major league teams interested in signing me. Bonus offers of $15,000, $20,000, and $30,000 were coming in. The Cubs were the jackpot and offered me $50,000 my senior year. My dad asked what I planned to do with the money and I told him I'd picked out a new convertible.

He wasn't too impressed with that answer.

My brother Frank was a good baseball player, too. I had heard that he had been offered a nice bonus to play professional ball, but my father wanted Frank to go to college and never let the scouts talk to him. Back then scouts talked to the coaches and then parents. Frank played catcher at the University of Kentucky for a couple of years, only to come home and find out that he might have had a chance to play pro baseball. Naturally, he was upset at my father for not telling him about those visiting scouts.

The divorce and scouting situation had caused a rift with Frank, so my dad stayed out of the decision about whether I should play pro baseball or college football. So we had a meeting and I talked it over with my mom and brothers, and their vote was simple and unanimous: They all wanted me to go to college. Bob had simply asked Mom what she wanted and when she said college, he slammed his fist down like a judge with a gavel.

"That's it. You go to college."

It wasn't what I wanted to hear, but at that time, we still did what we were told.

The basketball court was another sanctuary for me. I could handle the ball well enough to play guard, and even had the ability to dunk. I was also lucky enough to be elected a co-captain. Most of the players on the team, including Linwood, were kids from the Lower End like me. They might've had a different color skin, but I didn't notice, as we'd often played together growing up. Sports and schools had always been integrated in Beaver Falls.

We used to scale up to the second floor of the high school and walk across a six-inch ledge to pry open a window and slip into the gym on Sundays to play. As youngsters we had used the same method to sneak into games without paying. It was a small town, most everybody knew each other, and a policeman standing at the entrance of the gym bet me that I couldn't sneak past him. I went in through the window and came up behind him asking for my nickel. He gave it to me and then kicked me out and made me pay to get back in!

It wasn't until a new coach was hired that I decided to leave basketball behind. This was an old-school coach, the sort who never smiled, and our styles didn't align. As a team, we knew how to run, but he wanted to play slow-down basketball. One time early in the season he pulled me out of the game and I never made it to the bench. A teammate threw me a towel and I kept walking to the locker room. A couple of minutes later I heard footsteps as Benny Singleton, the co-captain, followed me. He'd also quit. Besides altar boy practice, this was the only thing I had ever quit, and I'm not proud of it to this day.

Anyway, I had other activities to fall back on. Even though it wasn't at the top of my list, football was an important part of my life. Growing up, our town was a football mecca. Every Friday in the fall, the stands would be packed and a loose gang of kids from our end of town always walked to games, making the two-mile trek up to Reeves Stadium at Geneva College.

And when we weren't playing or going to local games, my friends and I made up our own, which was something I had always done with Frank. A football and baseball were relatively expensive items back then, so we improvised in a pinch. Nobody had a bucket of regulation baseballs in their garage. Instead we'd roll newspaper up until it resembled a stiff, rectangular hot dog. The newspaper "balls" were not even close to symmetrical and you could watch them roll and curve unpredictably in the air as they whizzed by. Frank threw some of the most wicked curveballs I'd ever seen with those things. We'd also stay up at night sewing up old socks so they'd resemble a baseball.

To be sure, though, there was no little brother sympathy shown in those backyard games. Next door to us was an abandoned two-story building that had housed the local laundry, and where you hit the ball off its wall determined if it was a single, double, triple, or home run. If we got a ball onto the roof, we shimmied up an exterior exposed pipe to retrieve our homemade contraptions. Frank loved beating me, but he also appreciated seeing me nail one of his pitches.

Learning how to watch and anticipate the rolled newspaper cone's quick and unpredictable movements, waiting until the right moment, surely helped me develop a good batter's eye and generate speed on my swing.

When Frank pitched to me, he'd sometimes dress me up in catcher's equipment, while the back of our house—which was a narrow, two-story, white frame house—made for the perfect backstop; there was only one window in that part of the house on the second level, so unless a pitch was incredibly wild, we didn't run the risk of breaking any glass. One of my brothers had also set up a makeshift basketball hoop on a telephone pole in the alley by our house on the sidewalk. It was built to prop against telephone poles so we could move it to another that had a light on it when the day got dark. The street was uneven and there were potholes, but in winter we'd shovel the snow off the sidewalk, cut the fingers off our gloves, and play on the more even frozen ground. As a kid, when it was too cold outside, I went down into the basement and practiced dribbling with Linwood, counting down the days until Beaver Falls thawed out.

* * *

Nothing, however, needed to thaw out in Florida that January of 1969 when we played in the third AFL/NFL World Championship game. At around nine in the morning we had a team breakfast in a private room. After we ate there was a general meeting with the entire team and coaching staff. Before we even arrived in Florida, Weeb already knew how he wanted us to play, so we had the mental part of the game down pat before we got into town.

Coach Ewbank addressed the team, and the mood was one of trying to pretend it was a normal game. Weeb had been there ten years before, when he coached the Baltimore Colts to victory in an NFL Championship Game against the New York Giants, so he knew what worked. He tried his best to keep everything routine, especially down to the practices all week long in Florida. He didn't even enforce a curfew until two days before the game.

Weeb broke us up into offense and defense groups, and we touched base before being dismissed. I took a walk on the beach, wanting some quiet time. But there were people around, so I made my way back to my room to be alone.

You never know when it might rain in Florida, but it was still dry as we stepped outside into the Galt parking lot, where three buses sat idling. There were only forty players maximum on a team back then, usually split between two buses, but we had an extra one for family and administrative personnel. I headed toward the players' bus on the far left, and my knees were feeling good as they'd been aspirated the day before. My right one was drained once a week following what was then an "experimental" surgery I had in 1965. The Jets team doctor, who had operated only a few days after co-owner and president Sonny Werblin had introduced me to the media, declared the operation a triumph. Doc Nicholas met me post-surgery with Mr. Werblin and said, "Joe, I think you can play four years." Four years later to the month, I had two other knee surgeries, but I was still able to drop back and set up to throw, break out of the pocket and run on occasion, spin and hand off, all of which was enough to help win games—and board the bus.

The gentle hum of the air-conditioning was the only noise I remember as I walked down an aisle separating seats filled with some of the most talented athletes on the planet. For away games, one of the two New York Jets team buses usually left for the stadium an hour earlier, bringing in the players who needed extra taping, knees drained, kinks worked out of legs and backs and shoulders. This time we all went together.

Getting ready for a game, especially if you had a nagging injury, could take some time. If you were a veteran, respect and usually a more beaten body got you a good spot in line. There's a head trainer and a couple assistants and they're standing there with rolls of tape and scissors, just wrapping and taping for two hours. Some players are picky and like the way a certain trainer tapes so they wait for him, others are just first come, first served. If they were doing your knee then you would stand on the table so the trainer would be eye-level with what he taped. Our head trainer, Jess Snedeker, had taped my knees every game since my rookie season.

My knee gave an annoying zap of pain as I sat down, but by this point the sting was just white noise, something that happened so often throughout the day that I barely noticed. I slumped into a window seat and stretched my legs to get comfortable. I extended them across the seat, waiting for my teammates to board the bus.

I looked out the window and thought about the strip of Florida beach I'd just walked down. The Galt in Fort Lauderdale had made for a fine base camp compared to the brutal winter slamming New York. Thirty-two degrees in that city whereas Florida felt tropical. I was used to heat and humidity, but Florida felt luxurious compared to my college days at Alabama in August.

Tuscaloosa took some getting used to, boy. I had never

felt weather like that—hot, humid, and heavy with that distinct smell of the paper mill. Have you ever smelled a paper mill? It's near putrid, like rotten eggs. A sulfur stink. You've got to get used to it. The factory was maybe five miles northwest of campus and wasn't a bad place beyond the stench. I worked there one summer, loading trucks and boxcars, stacking bales and reams of paper. The labor was like going to the gym, and back then none of us were even lifting weights. There wasn't even a weight room at school.

Once the bus doors closed, I took out an apple. By four bites I was down to the core. Winston Hill took a seat and leaned back. Jim Hudson sat across from me and we nodded, neither of us in the mood to break the silence.

The regular nine p.m. team snack the night before a game had been subdued as well. Some guys were more tightly wound than others, and nobody wanted anybody going off on anybody, so we were all aware of not rubbing each other the wrong way. We enjoyed the sense of ritual that made us focus and leave the outside stuff outside. It was a football family, so to speak.

Now we were pulling out of the Galt parking lot, engine humming. I'd been through the process in one form or another for most of my playing life at that point, but had never put much thought into the bus ride itself. The card games and cursing that come with losing and the laughing that comes with winning. Somebody's portable radio turning from static to station as the team voted on songs with either cheers or groans. Players and equipment managers and trainers chattering, shouting over each other, digging deep into bags of chewing tobacco, drinking sodas, smoking. There was a sense of camaraderie that came out of trips with that much ego and talent compressed into a rolling tin can.

Busting a teammate's chops and wisecracking on each other was normal. But this silence also felt natural. More than natural—a necessity right then. There were a couple of world-class chop busters on that 1968 team, but this time all was calm. Our Jets hadn't made it this far before and now we were rolling toward the biggest game of our lives, less than four hours from running out onto the field. Forty-one million people were going to watch how that destiny would play out—even though I had already "guaranteed" it.

I later saw a clip on TV that said I had supposedly given the guarantee to Johnny Sample, our defensive captain. There was Johnny on the news saying, "Joe came up to me in my room and said he guarantees that we're going to win the game."

And I should point out that Johnny, easily one of the cleverest trash talkers to play the game, plays it up, asking, "Joe! How can you say that?"

He tells the reporter that I'd simply shrugged and said, "That's the way I feel."

The way I remember it, there had been a dinner at the Miami Springs Villas, one of the area's busiest banquet houses. Three nights before the game, the Miami Touchdown Club had hosted an awards dinner where Colts QB Earl Morrall received the NFL Player of the Year and I got the AFL Player of the Year. This wasn't some big event I'd been planning a speech for, to me it was just another team function Ramos was dragging me to. So there I am at the podium accepting my trophy, when some jerk in the back of the room yells out, "Hey, Namath, we're going to kick your ass!"

I cut him off. "Whoa, whoa! Wait a minute, buddy. I've got news for you. We're gonna win the game, I guarantee it." I was pissed, and the three or four hundred people in the room got pretty quiet. It was rude. The guy had interrupted me as I was accepting my award. I guess I should be grateful to him because he triggered my behavior and a reaction that created something that has been with us for the last fifty years, but I'm not.

I just said what I hoped our entire Jets team thought, except I framed it as a guarantee. I didn't even think about the comment. If it had been a big bold declaration at the awards ceremony, then you can sure bet Ramos would have stepped in to fix it. I think it was Edwin Pope who put it in his *Miami Herald* headline. But from then on, the media used the statement to stoke the fires before the big game. After all, this is entertainment, show business, as I learned.

Being in the newspaper had always been dicey for me. The first time was for baseball, in *The News Tribune,* which had covered the first Little League game of the season. I always grabbed the sports page, so when I saw my own name printed for the first time it was a huge deal through my nine-year-old eyes. I was a decent player and the local writer had been impressed that I'd gotten two solid hits out of four times at bat. The paper had arrived on our doorstep and I'd read and reread the article sitting on the floor, folding the sheet so it would be front and center when my brother Bob came home and I handed it to him.

Bob walked in the front door after I'd read it the tenth or

twelfth time. I proudly held it out to him, unable to stop a big toothy smile. "Look, I'm in the paper!"

He grabbed the carefully folded section and quickly read the small article. I watched his face in anticipation, naively waiting for his own proud smile.

"What happened?"

I'll tell you what happened, I thought as I imagined my two hits, which were growing in magnitude as I replayed them in my mind. I looked up at my older brother, ready to give him a play-by-play of my athletic prowess, but Bob's slightly bored face halted that highlight reel. It was such a stark contrast—the total opposite of his excitement that I had already imagined—that I was confused.

"What happened?" I repeated. "What do you mean?"

"Yeah," he said with a shrug. "You only got two hits out of four. What happened the other two times?"

My older brothers, my older sister, and the gritty, hard-working atmosphere of a steel town in Pennsylvania banged and beat down bravado. You could be proud, and determination and accomplishments were prized, but you held yourself a certain way, and in our house, my brothers made sure of that. Partly, I believe, because that's just the nature of most folks in that area, and also because Bob sure as hell wasn't going to miss a chance to torture his little brother; he watched my face fall as he handed the newspaper back to me with a bored expression but I just *knew* inside this was like Christmas morning to him.

I had been excited to show my whole family the article, but now I was thinking about those two other times at bat. At that age, I had already played sports long enough to not expect perfection, and that creative ability to make small adjustments, to learn, to adapt in the moment was what I loved about the constant challenge. I hadn't thought being in the newspaper made me better than anybody else, but my brother was just instilling, reinforcing, a long-standing respectful way to handle accomplishments. And it helped me shift focus to what I needed to improve rather than my achievements. My brothers were, again, twelve, nine, and six years older than me and they already thought I was spoiled, so they had no problem, were often eager even, to step in and balance things out. In our family and in Beaver Falls in general, confidence was fine, but cockiness just wasn't acceptable. And no, I wasn't being cocky about the article, but Bob must have sensed something close so he knocked me down a notch.

That was one of the earliest examples I remember of a lesson that runs through my life. I've been blessed with some great friends, doctors, teammates, coaches, and family members who taught me: It's not how you get knocked down that matters, it's how you get back up. I realize that's something of a cliché for most people. But for me it was a fundamental principle to live by. Because, let me tell you, I've had a lot of practice being knocked down—I'm a semi-expert at getting knocked down.

CHAPTER THREE

So I settled into my seat, thinking about the beach and how quiet the bus was, when I also remembered that I'd given my two free tickets to Bob and Dad to come to the game that afternoon. The two free Super Bowl tickets saved me a total of twenty-four dollars. The thought made me happy, but it didn't cut through the quietness of the bus. I was looking out the window, not seeing anything, but beginning to appreciate the upcoming challenge to achieve my dream. I had made the team and now had an opportunity to win the championship. I wasn't thinking about how our team was expected to lose or were perceived as laughably lucky to have even made it this far. Sportswriters had seemed to run out of verbs to describe the devastation the Baltimore Colts were about to bring down on us. The Vegas odds put us as a pathetic eighteen-point underdog.

The name-calling didn't just end with us. The entire American Football League was generally viewed as second rate to the National Football League. The NFL had the longer history, the tradition, the straitlaced crew-cut image, while the AFL had the energy of our generation behind it, and I wasn't cutting my hair or shaving my mustache to lead the charge. The Jets organization respected the sport and the athletes, but the top dogs knew football had to be entertaining to thrive.

Well, I was at dinner with one such top dog, president and co-owner Mr. Sonny Werblin and his wife. I was frustrated and complaining about something being written about the team and me when Mrs. Werblin, a professional singer before she married, just looked at me and said, "Joe, it's show business, honey."

Enraged, I pounded the table and almost raised my voice "This isn't show business! It's football!"

Clearly amused by my innocent ignorance, she chuckled and smiled. "It's show business. It's entertainment."

The AFL took the sport of football itself just as seriously, but they also had the understanding that it had to be watchable, and for that you needed stars, personalities, and faces to get people interested and following the players behind the masks.

In 1963, Mr. Werblin, Leon Hess, Townsend Martin, Phil Iselin, and Donald Lillis bought the Titans of New York from team founder Harry Wismer, who had started the Titans with the rest of the original AFL in the 1960 season. I never knew Mr. Wismer, but he had been a radio announcer in the 1940s and 1950s and parlayed that into ownership. The Titans had experienced cash-flow problems, which forced Wismer to sell. Some of the original Titans still on the team—namely Don Maynard, Larry Grantham, and Bill Mathis—were with me on the bus, and they had told training camp stories about the old paychecks bouncing as high as basketballs.

Mr. Hess, Mr. Werblin, and the others paid $1 million in 1963 for the Titans. (The Jets are now valued at more than a billion dollars.) Mr. Werblin immediately set out rebranding the team. He named them the Jets to capitalize on the sex appeal of the gang from the great musical *West Side Story* and parlay the hype of the Jet Era into the team. He hired former NFL championship–winning coach Weeb Ewbank to give the team a solid foundation as coach and general manager. Finally, he moved the team's home field from the old Polo Grounds to newly built Shea Stadium in 1964.

Mr. Werblin was quickly starting a feud with the beloved and storied New York Giants by establishing the legitimacy of the Jets. Things really took off, though, when he used his entertainment connections to negotiate a television deal for the AFL with NBC. Mr. Werblin grew up in Flatbush, Brooklyn, and attended Rutgers University. He started at Music Corporation of America in 1932 and moved up to president by 1951. MCA became the biggest talent agency in show business, and Mr. Werblin was known as the "World's Greatest Agent" before eventually leaving in 1962. Thirty years later, not only did he develop TV and radio shows, but he personally handled stars like Ed Sullivan, Jackie Gleason, Alfred Hitchcock, and Jack Benny among hundreds of greats of the day. He was a star maker and could be a network breaker if he wanted. (He moved Benny and a package of entertainers from NBC to CBS in 1949.) Long story short, that television deal quickly put the AFL and NFL on a level playing field, so to speak, by bringing games from *both* leagues to living rooms across the country.

But the NFL was perceived as an elite league and they

proved it during the past two championship games. In the first one, the NFL Green Bay Packers beat the AFL Kansas City Chiefs 35–10. The following year, the Packers beat the AFL's Oakland Raiders 33–14.

And now it was our turn. On the bus, driving to the Orange Bowl stadium, we all knew the ability we had as a team, but that still didn't change the fact that the NFL had emphatically won both times the two leagues went toe-to-toe. But we also felt like Kansas City didn't play their best in the first, and Oakland was off in the second.

To me, when I was thinking about playing pro ball, I didn't separate the leagues. In fact, a lot of the AFL teams had players who were cut from NFL teams, such as Maynard and Johnny Sample, two of our stars. I watched the AFL on television in Beaver Falls growing up and right on through to college. So when it came to league reputation, I didn't care what other people thought—I could see Lance Alworth was special on the San Diego Chargers. I could see Bobby Bell was something, too, at his linebacker position with the Kansas City Chiefs. Alworth ended up in the Hall of Fame, I should mention. Yes, indeed, the AFL had players. Cookie Gilchrist? Shoot, Cookie was outrageous, a great running back. He was slick. He was fun. And he was about six-foot-four, with a big head and gigantic shoulders but he could sure pick up his feet—man, he was quick and strong.

The AFL had ball players, all right. And they also started the draft war in a way, so that each league was trying to poach players and inflate the numbers, with the bidding going back and forth. The AFL could play, but they didn't have bragging rights because they hadn't won the big one yet. If we didn't pull this one out, then we'd have to wait another year for the two leagues to go at it.

We, of course, also wanted to win the game for ourselves, our team, and our city, but there was a sense of responsibility here to reshape our league in the public's mind. Three defeats in a row and you're out, come on. And we were already out according to the bookies and the writers. We'd heard a rumor that one of the Colts players had already spent his championship bonus money fixing his house up.

Contemplating such things, I watched the highway roll past. It had been almost ten minutes of utter silence when our punter, Curley Johnson, a thick veteran who had been with the Jets since 1961—when they were still called the Titans of New York—showed why he was one of our leaders. He was also the funniest guy on the team by far, in addition to being a backup tight end, wide receiver, fullback, and halfback. Rosters were much smaller back then and guys played what they could when needed, and Curley was a roly-poly jack-of-all-trades. He had these folksy sayings for every sort of circumstance. Things would just drop out of his mouth that broke up the entire locker room. Whenever guys started messing around, putting on a show, Curley took it as his time to shine. He'd come out on his knees with a pillow stuffed under his shirt imitating Weeb, our head coach, who, by the way, would be in the audience. A lot of humor anywhere Curley was, and comedic relief can be a powerful thing.

Addressing nobody in particular, Curley angled his head up and said in his Texas drawl that stretched words like taffy: "Chicken ain't nothin' but a bird."

The silence crackled with energy as we all digested what he had just uttered. I looked away from the window and thought, *What? What in the heck did I just hear?*

Nobody said anything. Just more silence that Curley felt the need to break, so once again, slightly louder: "Chicken ain't nothin' but a bird."

He said it again, even louder, elongating "bird," and the tension broke, as every single person on that bus started laughing and giving shouts of agreement, forcefully releasing a wave of emotion. The bus went from pensive silence to rollicking enthusiasm and joy.

"That's damn right, you know it, Curley," I said.

"A game's a game, man," I heard somebody shout over the laughing in front of me.

"Nothing but another game!" somebody up front shouted.

"Chicken ain't nothin' but a bird!"

We might've been doubled over roaring at Curley's line, but man we desperately needed a release.

It *was* a damn big game, but still the same one we'd played all season long together. And I'd had experiences with big games, beginning with my first college start against the University of Georgia, way back in 1962, when I was just a sophomore. I can hear Ray Charles now...

* * *

The entire summer, we were all focused on that first Georgia game, even though I wasn't sure I was Alabama's starting quarterback. There were three QBs returning from the '61 championship team—Jack Hurlbut, Mal Moore, and Carlton Rankin—and I was the new kid along with fellow freshman Buddy French .

Coach Paul "Bear" Bryant didn't have depth charts. Teams wore different color jerseys during practice, and that told us all we needed to know. The red was the first team, the white second, the blue third, the orange fourth, and the yellow jerseys were the injured guys. One of the great lessons I learned from my high school coach was that I couldn't control anything other than my performance in a competition, so I went hard, quick, and fast— on every single play. I never just went through the motions. In 1962 I wasn't verbal, as a leader I generally wasn't much of a talker. Three older brothers had taught me to keep my mouth shut. I maintained a lower profile, so my execution on the field was my only chance of seeing playing time.

Although with Coach Bryant up in a tower peering down on us, allowing him to scan his five fields at once as he watched practice—I couldn't imagine doing anything less. He demanded full speed and made sure we were moving nearly the entire practice. We did very little standing around. And I know all my teammates would agree with me on this: Each of us was *convinced* the man in the tower had his eyes on our every move. Coaches, too. You knew he was up there, and that alone made me too paranoid not to go full speed.

By the spring game, the starting quarterback position was narrowed down to three of us. I knew I had played well enough, but nobody had been told who was starting in the fall. Then, during the last week of practice before the first game, I went to the cage where one of the equipment managers gave me my basket with socks, jockstrap, T-shirt, and crimson jersey. That was how I knew I would be practicing with the first unit. But even then, the starting position was in jeopardy until I ran out on that field on gameday. It was never locked in and I never took it for granted.

When it came time to hand out numbers my freshman year, I was given 12. At Alabama, players didn't ask for numbers. But once I realized Pat Trammell had worn the same number during his National Championship season, I felt honored to put those digits on—especially that first varsity game, which would happen at Birmingham's Legion Field.

If we were playing a game that drew more fans, the teams played on Legion Field, around fifty miles northeast of our campus. When we played there, we traveled up the day before and had a workout on the field. Then we checked into our hotel for the night. The next day we had our pregame meal at the hotel. This was my first stroll with Coach Bryant and his other quarterbacks. Being my first start, I'd never done this with him before. So, there are five of us walking around the block, and Coach Bryant hadn't said a word for a while. We're kind of following along with him, hanging back a bit.

Coach Bryant sucks in a lungful of his Chesterfield or Pall Mall and says, "Joe, you got the plan?"

Pause.

"Yes, sir. I think so."

Have you ever wondered how he got the nickname Bear Bryant? Some might attribute it to his being six-five, but from my understanding it was actually because he was rumored to have wrestled a bear at a carnival. I certainly wasn't going to ask him. I tend to think that whoever first branded him that did so in a situation like mine, where he paused and suddenly looked like a towering grizzly bear.

"You *think so*?" he growled. His words cut right through me. "Damn, son, it's time you *know*. The hay is in the barn."

I had no idea what he was talking about. *Hay? Barn? What eats hay? Horses? How does it get into a barn? Are we talking about tractors?*

Coach's eyes locked on mine and I said, "Yes, sir!" And then to make it clear I understood, I repeated it with emphasis. "Yes, sir!"

That was a lesson that I kept through every professional game. I made sure I convinced myself that I was ready. I studied. I learned. I wanted to be absolutely sure I was ready for what was going to happen, and if I was surprised, I'd have the ability to adjust.

I wasn't adjusting too well and had never felt that much pressure going onto a field. I was a sophomore starting on a defending National Championship team. An hour before my first start, I was in the locker room and my temples were throbbing, an annoying pounding pain. I was too nervous to say anything and I sure as heck wasn't going to complain. Then the quarterback coach came over. "All right, let's go!" I got up with the other QBs and followed the coach out.

If the pounding didn't stop, I wouldn't be allowed to play. We walked down the ramp, got to the edge of the field, and as we started going onto it, I heard the roar of tens of thousands of fans, just as the band started playing "Dixie" and "Yea Alabama."

I didn't even feel my headache anymore. Gone. The pain just evaporated. But I still had the nerves, man. Too many volts were running through my system. I was nervous even warming up. The stands were packed. The adrenaline carried over to after the kickoff and my first huddle. I felt a bit out of control and needed to settle in, so for my first varsity play I called a quarterback sneak, the safest play in the book. The first play of my career. Why did I call it? Because I needed it! I needed to get hit. I needed that jolt to help reset and calm my nervous system down. And you can bet that the players on the other side were more than happy to oblige.

Alabama and Coach Bryant hold such a special place for me. The entire thirteen years of my pro career, all the way through 1977, I returned to Tuscaloosa to train.

Hay in the barn. Chicken ain't nothin' but a bird. Coach Bryant would have loved Curley.

Curley knew what we needed, definitely what I needed. Chicken ain't nothin' but a bird and a game is just a game, another game. After that, the bus never felt flat. We were loose, we were together, and that is how you want to go into a championship game.

CHAPTER FOUR

At my kitchen table, I'm watching this broadcast and the first thing that comes to mind is, boy, has television come a long way since 1969. The second is the sky at the Super Bowl. It was still gray, but the field had decent footing considering the rain from the night before. Field conditions had been a contributing factor to my first right knee injury.

But it felt good going into the Super Bowl. Well, "good" is a relative term, which for me meant no sharp pains slicing through my joint when I walked, no instability that made my right knee cave inward. My knees…crazy how they feel so much better now. I guess that's a perk of having them both replaced in 1992. You see, I never had a problem with them before a game against North Carolina State in October 1964.

That day, at least three carloads of family and friends from Beaver Falls had driven down to Tuscaloosa. It was gameday morning outside the Moon Winx Lodge, where the team stayed, and I went out into the parking lot to say hi. One of the guys said, "Hey, Joe, you guys are nineteen-point favorites. What do you think?"

I looked at him. "That's a lot of points, but don't bet against us."

North Carolina State was good, and we were both undefeated at that point. We shut them out 21–0, but I didn't have a lot to do with it. Steve Sloan, our junior quarterback, led the team to victory.

It was a third-and-2. We needed two yards to get a first down. I had called a run-pass option around the right end. I got the snap, started sprinting to my right, and when I planted my right foot to cut upfield to run for the first down, my right knee caved in. Boom. I just went down. And it hurt. I walked off the field with some help and stayed on the sidelines. My knee swelled and the trainers took my pants off and put the ice packs on. We went to the hospital right after the game, and when they aspirated it with a needle that looked big enough to use on horses, there was blood swirling around in the liquid. If the fluid is a clear yellowish color, then it may not be a severe knee injury, but if there's red, you know something is torn. But there were no MRIs or anything to provide a detailed overview of the injury. It came down to "how much does it hurt?"

When we looked at my shoes afterward, the cleats on the edges were bent out in different directions, so I must have hit a hole or an uneven spot. But the trainer also hypothesized that my charley horse from the week earlier, the bruise on my thigh, might have weakened the muscles around my knee.

So I ended up hurting it three more times in practice throughout the season, never knowing exactly what was wrong; we just drained it and taped it for stability and got me onto the field so I could move around gingerly, still practicing plays until the swelling took me out. The ligaments were so wrecked that I never knew what might bring that flare of pain or where I'd be.

The last time it gave out, in 1965, right before the Orange Bowl in Miami against the Texas Longhorns, I was taking luggage out of a car trunk, twisted it a little too much, became a little unbalanced, and the knee caved in and the sharp pain let me know that I'd reinjured it. I didn't run or plant during practice that week. I wasn't expecting to play, but they taped me up just in case. As we were lined up on the sideline right before the national anthem, Coach Bryant was to my left, and he turned his head to our trainer, Jim Goostree, on my right. "Jim, can he play?"

Coach Goostree, surprised, looked at me and said, "I think so, Coach."

Starting quarterback Steve Sloan hurt his knee in the second half. We had been down but came back, and on the deciding play, one yard away from the winning touchdown, I called the quarterback sneak. I carried the ball, thought I'd crossed the plane, and the linesman on the right gave the touchdown signal. But the line judge on our offensive left came running in and said I hadn't. The officials conferred and the referee ruled no touchdown, Texas ball. If it had counted, we would have won.

A lot of football fans have come up to me over the years and said, "Joe, you scored on that play! I've watched replays."

My response has always been the same: "I was over the goal line, but I didn't score." We've gotta live with it. There weren't instant replays back then and there aren't replays in life, so deal with it.

I ended up playing that game, the last of my college time

with Alabama, in the same stadium that hosted this Super Bowl.

* * *

My knee was hurt, but professional athletes and teams just dealt with injuries differently. I didn't even have a real physical with the Jets before I signed. They knew I had a bad knee, but their doctors didn't look at it until I was officially a Jet. If you taped it enough, you added some stability, so if you didn't make a false step or misstep planting, didn't put that much pressure on the joint in a lateral movement, it held up okay. Even though we lost the game, I played well enough in the Orange Bowl for the Jets to take a chance.

This was also the first nationally televised prime-time collegiate bowl game. It had been organized in part by Mr. Werblin through his friendship with the heads of NBC. He believed in the star system and put effort into making professional athletes more like celebrities. He was quoted as saying "Stars sell tickets," and he promoted me as the Jets' star out of the gate. The day after the Orange Bowl, he had held a press conference in Miami, announcing that he had given me a record-breaking rookie contract.

Then I drove to Mobile, Alabama, for the Senior Bowl, the biggest college all-star game at that time, in my new British-racing-green Lincoln Continental with a white convertible top that Mr. Werblin had delivered at the Orange Bowl. It was no coincidence that it matched the Jets colors.

It's hard to believe that the Jets took the risk of allowing me to play in another game, potentially re-injuring or worsening my knee. But they did. And the day after that, the Jets flew me to New York City and Mr. Werblin personally introduced me to the media and socialites at Toots

Shor's Restaurant. But I still had a bad wheel. I didn't know if I could even continue playing. And I still hadn't had a physical! My first with the team doctor, though, would certainly be one to remember. It took place during the get-together. I was talking to Howard Cosell and Dave Anderson from the *New York Times* when a man came up to me and introduced himself, "Hello, Joe, my name is Dr. Nicholas, I'm the Jets' orthopedic surgeon."

I lit up and said, "How do you do, sir?"

"I hear you have a bad knee."

"Yes, sir."

"Well, I'd like to look at it."

"Yes sir. Anytime."

"Right now works." He took my arm and led me to the men's restrooms.

It was empty, and he stopped in the middle of the room. I unbuckled my pants and he knelt down on one knee and began manipulating my right leg.

Just then a guy walked in. He saw Dr. Nicholas bent down in front of me with my pants down and then looked up at me. He swiveled and made a U-turn right back out.

Without missing a beat, Dr. Nicholas said, "I've got to get in there for a better look. I'll see you at Lenox Hill Hospital tomorrow."

I walked out needing some time to process everything. I left Toots' with my friend and agent Mike Bite and the Jets offensive line coach, Chuck Knox, and we walked a few blocks in the snow until finding a quiet bar. I needed a drink with my thoughts and friends to share them with. Life was happening.

The next day Dr. Nicholas had me at Lenox Hill for pre-op

prep. His mom stopped by to visit me and gave me a St. Jude necklace. I consider St. Jude a close pal—I'd actually already prayed to the saint of hopeless causes, or as I renamed it "difficult tasks," as a child to help me grow taller. It got me thinking…what did she know that I didn't? But I believed St. Jude could only help. I put it on and still wear one to this day.

Forty-eight hours after walking out of Toot Shor's, Dr. Nicholas operated on my knee for the first time. It was a mess—torn medial ligament, torn anterior and posterior cruciate ligament, chewed-up medial cartilage—and he removed a small cyst behind my knee. And since this was showbiz, a photographer for *Sports Illustrated,* Mike Bite, and the Jets' Frank Ramos all crowded into the room during surgery. When the doctor punctured the cyst, fluid shot across the room, and Mike watched as Ramos passed out.

"Oh, he hit the deck," Mike said, laughing.

Back then, it was primitive, brutal even, for cutting-edge surgeons like Dr. Nicholas. When I was finally able to leave the hospital, I'd lost twenty-seven pounds. They put my leg in an ankle-to-groin cast with a hole in the side so when I flexed my quad, synovial fluid shot out like a dog taking a leak. My Alabama roommate, Butch Henry, had a knee surgery earlier, and they'd left a hole in his knee the size of a dime to drain it.

I'd say Ramos got the last laugh though, because a week after surgery, he came into my room with a football, shoulder pads, and my Jets jersey and held them up. "Joe, the show must go on."

He got me up and helped me into the hallway with my crutches where they put on the pads and jersey. They leaned me against the wall, handed me the ball, and I posed for my first Topps card.

I hobbled out of the hospital a few days later with my swollen knee and a surreal sense of what my life was like now. I may have been rich compared to how I lived two weeks before, but I only knew how to live one way. The Jets hadn't assigned anybody to help me, so I asked the hospital to call me a taxi. I thanked all my nurses and got into the back, my leg in a plaster cast stretched across the seat as the driver took me to the airport.

After an uncomfortable flight back to Birmingham, Alabama, I was greeted by Mike Bite, who had driven my car that I'd left behind after the Senior Bowl three weeks earlier. If anybody was watching me get into the car, that would have been some entertainment. I had to get in the passenger side and slide across to get my right leg on the front seat, and use my left foot for the gas and brake to drive sixty miles back to Tuscaloosa and my old campus.

I had a few people ask why I was driving myself if I had to go through all that trouble. And yes, some of it had to do with Mike's driving, but it could've been anyone and I would've driven. I like the freedom of being in control and able to call my own shots. But I've also never let injuries hold me back on or off the field, whenever physically possible. Once, my teammate John Dockery invited me out to his house on Long Island. I still had a hip-to-toe plaster cast but felt up for it. I flew in on a seaplane, and not until I was climbing into the waiting rowboat did it occur to me that one slip and it'd all be over. Driving sounds safer now, doesn't it?

The university always offered me a reliable sense of routine. I still had some courses to take that spring, but a class like "History of the Christian Church" was up three stories of stairs in Woods Hall. It took me over twenty minutes to swing my casted leg around and take one stair at a time with the assistance of crutches, but the real adventure was the descent. Negotiating stairs with a cast and crutches was literally life threatening, and I dropped the class.

I became obsessed with my new goal: regaining leg strength and mobility. It was tough dealing with an injury, but I found it easier once I had a game plan. Alabama trainer Jim Goostree guided me through my rehab routine, and there wasn't much to it other than straight leg and side leg lifts. Also, I'd lay on my belly and lift a weighted boot. He'd make me lift until my whole body was trembling, about to give out. Alabama was kind enough to let me use their facilities and I stayed there almost right up until I was set to move to New York City for the start of the Jets' training camp.

* * *

But my knee felt good going into this World Championship four years later. Weeb, our coach, had told us that we should handle this like any other away game. We weren't going to break any traditions or habits. He trusted what we had always done. So we'd stayed in New York maintaining our regular practice schedule. Then, a week before the kickoff, we arrived in Fort Lauderdale and practiced in Marlin Stadium, where the legendary New York Yankees team had spring training.

Weeb always found a wise way to retain balance with the team. He wasn't one of those chair-throwing hotheads; he'd listen to you, but he was still coach—and a damn good one at that. He's the only coach, in fact, to win both an NFL and AFL championship, an accomplishment that'll never be broken. Weeb liked to start our normal workday at noon. His theory was to practice as close as possible to the one p.m. start time for our games. That schedule also afforded me the opportunity to enjoy the New York nightlife and still get my eight hours of sleep. It also allowed some of my teammates to have second jobs, like Billy Mathis, who worked as a stockbroker before coming to practice.

By 1969, I had warmed up to some of the perks of being a pro ball player, but the initial move to New York City in 1965 had been painful. Things hadn't gone as well as I would have liked, because I wasn't practicing or playing all that great. I struggled throughout the six preseason games. I was a backup to start with, and I didn't play in the opening game of my rookie season.

Expectations were also high, even from me. But I just wasn't meeting them. I was a different player. My knee was still recovering and my body was still compensating for the injury. I couldn't run near as well as I could before the injury. I was lost, man. I can remember being alone, living on 86th Street, and just walking around by myself after practice, trying to process things.

But that changed over the year as my play improved and I made friends. New York became my second home and the newspapers began printing the activities of "Broadway Joe." I'm not complaining, mind you. And by the way, that nick-name, "Broadway Joe," came from the *Sports Illustrated* with me on the cover. I was a rookie, and tried to stay quiet out of respect for the veterans, and being a cover boy was a little uncomfortable, embarrassing even. There was some resent-ment that I was a "bonus baby," getting a lot more money than any other player and now there I was on the cover of a magazine looking clean. Hey, I appreciated it, but it made me feel awkward.

Following a practice at Shea, we walked back into the locker room and each player's stool had a *Sports Illustrated* on it with yours truly on the cover. I hadn't seen it before and was surprised and mortified at seeing my smiling face. Some players chuckled and others muttered not the nicest things about rookies as they threw the magazine toward the trash.

Our senior leader and offensive tackle, Sherman Plunkett, was sitting directly across the room from me looking at the magazine. He looked up at me, looked down at the magazine, back up at me, and with this great big smile on his face said, "Ole Broadway, Broadway Joe." Man, that made me feel better about it. And to this day I nearly always think of Sherman whenever I hear the nickname.

And it sure stuck.

But the attention wasn't always met with affection. Earlier in training camp there was an incident on the practice field, and rookie or not, I had to have my say. We had been doing laps and Wahoo McDaniel—a linebacker whose wrestling name was Chief Wahoo—had been clowning around, and he ran up behind me and jumped on my back and I fell down.

He was not a small guy. Everybody else just kept running around me. I got back up and finished my laps, and after practice we had one of our regular team meetings and one of the captains asked if anybody else had anything to add. I felt compelled to speak out, to say my piece. Enough was enough.

I stood up, maybe some of the guys thought I was going to ask everybody to give me a chance or something like that. But I got up and looked around the room.

"I have to tell you guys this. I'm here to play ball," I said.

"I want to help you win and I want to win. I'm here to work out there on the practice field, and if you want to mess with me, do it now and we'll fight. You might beat my ass, but you'll get a fight. Don't mess with me on the field."

That was it. Nobody jumped on my back after that. Plenty of guys on that team could have kicked my ass, but I was being honest; they would have to fight. They might think I was some spoiled rookie, but I grew up on the Lower End of Beaver Falls. I'd been taught to stand up for what I felt was right. You don't back down. Coach Bryant put that to the test 'cause nobody lasted long on the Crimson Tide if you backed down. The bottom line is I'll respect you, but you need to respect me. And I'd always been that way.

* * *

My childhood house was on Sixth Street, otherwise known as the Lower End of town. We'd play tackle football in the backyard with other crews from the neighborhood and Seventh Street south. There was also a housing project two blocks north by the railroad tracks, and they had a neighborhood football team and a field. We'd go there and you'd just play every position possible to stop the other team.

White, black, Hungarian, Jewish, it didn't matter. Racism might've been around my whole life, but not really being aware of it started out at home. We're talking about the social structure, and we're talking about getting along with one another, and how some people are biased, some people don't like the way somebody walks, they don't like the color of their skin. The way I was brought up with a mixed group of friends was the kind of outside-the-school education that became instinct, and I cherish it to this day.

I had never experienced much by way of segregation until I went to Alabama. When I arrived, I wasn't even aware the school was segregated and, if I had known, I probably wouldn't have gone. My best buddy growing up was black. Met him when I was four as he walked out of his house, which was directly across the street. I waved at him. Linwood Alford was also four at the time and he waved back. That was it. From that wave on, we were best friends, and he remains one of my dearest friends to this day. We immediately began hanging on a daily basis. We'd fish together, kick up dust racing down the road, knock on people's doors asking for empty soda or milk bottles to take back and return for pennies to buy candy.

My parents always made Linwood as welcome in our house as his mama made me feel in theirs. I hardly have a childhood memory without him in it. I'd sleep over at his place, and he'd sleep at mine. If Linwood was around at mealtime, there would be no questions, just another seat at our table. Like a lot of Europeans, my dad always kissed us as a good-bye and if "Linny," as my parents called him, was hanging out, then he got a farewell kiss, too.

Man, I loved Linwood. Still do, man. He made life so much more fun, and finally having somebody to run around with who was my age was a game changer. We made buddies with Freddy Manarino and Richie Rachael, two other kids from the block. I didn't even think about what to do with my free time 'cause Linwood and I would always find each other. We'd race down the street to the end of the block. If we saw somebody walk by with a pole and fishing tackle over their shoulder, we'd scramble to the garage and grab ours, and then run to catch up. By the time we reached the river, there would be half a dozen of us with our rods, ready to cast.

Dad was always encouraging me to fish, too, which was odd because I never once saw him touch a rod—not even when just the two of us went on a fishing trip in Ohio, over an hour away. He just really enjoyed watching me fish. Once he took me to a lake and it was raining. I mean it was pouring hard, man. Dumping down and we were getting soaked, but I wanted to get out there. Dad looked up at the dark clouds, shrugged, and rented us a rowboat from a very perplexed owner hiding from the rain in his shack. We rowed to the middle of the lake, obviously having it all to ourselves. Dad never touched a rod the whole time. He just sat there and watched as rain dripped off his hat. I can't remember if I even caught anything, but sitting in a boat in the rain with just Dad was one of my favorite moments with him. We packed up and went home like it had been a beautiful sunny day.

Not all the adults were as accommodating as him, though. I was around eight years old when Mom gave Linwood and me money to buy a slice of pizza at an Italian joint. I'd been there before and was talking to Linwood as we walked through the doors. The lady whose family owned the place looked at us in a way that immediately put me on alert. She'd always seemed nice before, but now she was clearly agitated.

"Namath, you can stay. You"—she gestured to Linwood—"get out of here!"

She said it with so much venom that it scared me. Her words bit and I was shocked at her sudden hatred and anger. I couldn't understand what she was talking about. Linwood simply turned and walked out and I followed him.

He didn't say anything, and I was still confused. I'd never seen an adult express such cruelty toward a child before.

It disturbed me, so that night I told my parents what happened. Mom saw how upset I was and explained it as gently as she could, saying that there are some people in this world who are so sad and angry that they find ways not to like other people. She never got into a discussion about race or brought up that it was about Linwood being black.

All my family thought that way, too. You were judged on your actions, and even Rita by then wouldn't hesitate to haul off and whip your butt if you crossed the line. There was only one big argument that I remember between Linwood and me, and I can't even remember what it was over, but we were both all hotheaded and it developed into a fistfight.

I had given him a straight shot right to the throat. He gasped and started making funny breathing sounds and dropped to his knees, unable to breathe. Rita saw what happened and ripped into me, right there as she bent down to help Linwood. In between making sure Linny could still breathe, she'd turn and yell at me. By then I was feeling horrible anyway. What did I just do to my best friend? She was my sister, but that didn't mean she was automatically going to take my side in a fight. I was kind of disappointed she was blaming me! I might have even held a grudge against her for making me feel so bad about it.

* * *

After only spending a short time at home that summer, I returned early to Alabama for my junior year in '63. I worked at the paper mill and had swapped out my seven-to-three shift for an eleven-to-seven shift. Students were well aware something was going on because the National Guard was making their presence known on campus. I'd seen military trucks and soldiers walking around. We'd heard rumors a few new black students were going to register at Foster Auditorium...which would break segregation for the first time in the history of the University of Alabama.

I walked up to the auditorium where I sometimes played basketball, and there was a crowd of maybe a couple hundred people. If you look at pictures, there is a man in a white shirt holding a camera, and I was standing near him. I was close enough to hear and see everything. As I listened to Alabama governor George Wallace's "Stand in the Schoolhouse Door" statement in support of his promise of "segregation now, segregation tomorrow, segregation forever," I looked at Vivian Malone. She and James Hood were the first black students to register. She seemed scared, and all I could think about was how brave she was. It was a heavy position to be in. She had poise.

I was so grateful President Kennedy had federalized the Alabama National Guard. I distinctly remember standing there watching a man in a suit to Governor Wallace's right say, "Step aside, Governor. This is now a federal issue." I still get goose bumps to this day thinking about that moment. I was around forty feet away watching their exchange as Wallace listened and remained in the doorway. I saw the emotions on Vivian's face as she waited and felt my own face surge with joy as she was *finally* escorted in to register for school. She officially broke segregation that day and taught us all a thing or two about inner strength.

Vivian ended up living in the same dorm as a girl I was dating, so we got to know each other. We'd talk about football and classes and laugh about Muhammad Ali, who was easily the most charismatic sports figure at the time, spouting funny little poems at press conferences. We weren't best friends by any means, but we knew each other's names and had conversations. I've met some of the most famous and powerful people in the world over the years, but I have to say few left the impression that knowing Vivian did. Just sitting there talking to her gave anybody a sense of her poise, kindness, and strength. It wasn't as if anger and racism ended once she enrolled, so she still had to deal with hostility as she went on to become the university's first black graduate in 1965.

Some people openly used the N-word around campus or at parties, but never on the field. Coach Bryant never said anything specifically to me about segregation or racism, but one time I saw him walking down the hallway when one of the janitors we all knew as Hoochman was mopping the floor. He was a black man, older than Coach Bryant, and Coach greeted Hoochman and they had a conversation. I can't remember what it was about, something casual, but I distinctly remember Coach Bryant nodding and saying, "Yes, sir. All right, I'll take care of it, Mr. Hooch." Over the years, I noticed that Coach, who offered the school's first scholarship to a black student in 1971, always addressed Hoochman as "sir" in every exchange they shared.

Even on the Jets, things weren't always smooth in that area and the ugliness would sometimes showcase itself. But to me, I came into that locker room sincerely believing in treating people with respect, compassion, and empathy. If you don't share the same belief system that I do, then that's your prerogative. We might get along in the workplace; however, we'd sure as heck keep our distance after practice.

* * *

But the good far outweighs the bad and there were so many good friends on that team, on that bus. You know, I don't remember much once we pulled into the stadium for the Super Bowl. We all had our routines for getting ready, and that day nothing was different. I undressed and got into my jock strap and shorts and T-shirt, slipping my feet into the black sandals I wore around the locker room and to the trainer's table. I do recall seeing Maynard walking around, limping slightly from his hamstring injury that we were keeping a tight lip about.

When I got to Jeff, our head trainer, he began a process that had long been mastered: taping my knees and ankles. By then, we knew exactly how tight to wrap, how much tape would provide the maximum support without losing flexibility and causing pain.

Then it was more tape over my socks because I'd get kicked in the ankle and sometimes even kick myself there, and it hurt like heck. The whole process took around fifteen minutes. I walked back into the locker room and sat on the bench. I turned on my portable stereo and tried to find James Brown, the Rolling Stones, Laura Nyro, Harry Belafonte, Janis Joplin, maybe some Glen Campbell. Looking down beside me at the clean stained wood, I missed the simple metal stools and cinder-block walls of our Shea Stadium. But that was luxury compared to the Denver Broncos rodeo stadium in '65. That was when I first wondered if I had made a mistake signing with the AFL instead of the NFL. The locker room floor was dirt, like the infield of a baseball park. The seats were rusty folding chairs, and we hung our clothes on a single nail hammered into the wall. Not here though! The Orange Bowl had beautiful weather, beautiful girls, and a beautiful locker room.

Above my locker, hand lettered in a green that matched the Jets' uniform, was number 12, a dot, and then NAMATH. The sign was perfectly coordinated with my custom-made white cleats, one of the most stylish gifts I'd ever received, from long-term head equipment manager Bill Hampton. Everybody on our team felt close to Hamp. Apparently, he'd spoken with Riddell, the company who made some of the players' cleats, explaining how I always, always taped my standard-issue black shoes with white tape before every practice and game. The joke around the locker room was that Weeb, who was tight with a buck and was also the general manager, complained about the cost of the tape that I used on my shoes. So why not just make the cleats white, too, so the whole shebang matched?

Hampton had a keen attention to detail, so much so that he'd even coordinated the stabilizing leather strip at the top of the lace holes to the Jets' signature green tint. The ones he ordered really popped, man! To my knowledge, nobody else in the league, nobody else in football, had white cleats back in 1968, and my prized gift had earned a couple of trash-talking quips on the field, but nothing too bad.

"Why not look sharp on the field?" I'd answer back.

Heck, I don't want to play like everybody else out there, and I sure don't want to look like everybody else out there. Sometimes I'd glance down at them on the field, and they'd give me a little spark of confidence, just like that white tape had done for me going all the way back to my senior year in college, when I'd started every game with the same taping ritual.

We called wrapping the white tape around my shoes "spatting," after the old dandies who wore white spats over their shoes. At most, we had only two pairs of shoes at Alabama, and as they wore out I began taping them for support—and I liked the look. It didn't occur to me that Coach Bryant might not appreciate this little extra flair. I did start to get worried when a teammate said, "Sheeeit, Joe, wait until Coach sees that tape job. He's gonna get yo ass. Puttin' all that tape around your shoe—he ain't gonna like it."

Initially, I never gave any thought to what other people might think about what I was doing with my shoes. I just liked the way they looked, so why not? And it wasn't just on the football field. I was always taking little things I saw and liked and adding them to whatever I was doing. During one of my off-season summer jobs, I had a foreman who always wore a clean, white T-shirt and Levi's jeans creased to perfection. Even his shoes and shoelaces were orderly. It amazed me—this guy had such style. Nobody I knew dressed like him, and we're talking about work boots, jeans, and a T-shirt. He was clean, sharp, so I asked about his shoelaces.

"I was in the military," he said. "There's a specific way to do everything there, and they taught us to lace shoes right over left."

"Man, that looks so spiffy," I said, and the next day I laced my shoes the same way and did the same with every pair of shoes I wore from there on to this day.

My dad also was a neat dresser, and Mom had her style with hats and knew enough for Woolworth's to eventually hire her to oversee buying ladies' wear for one of the biggest stores in Beaver Falls. Considering that background, you might not be surprised to learn that, like I mentioned, I started wrapping white tape around my specially laced cleats. Man, I loved my feet feeling secure, but I also got a kick out of how the all-white stood out on the field. It became a routine and while I wasn't superstitious, I didn't go out of my way to walk under a ladder.

So, no, Coach Bryant never said anything about my spatting. Didn't even scrutinize them once, from what I could tell. However, when I came in for a one-on-one meeting sporting a goatee, he sure did look at me funny. Summer break was starting and I had grown a little beatnik goatee. Each player at Alabama had to go in and share with Coach their summer plans. So I entered and he was sitting behind his desk. He looked up at me and just froze. Totally frozen and staring at my face like he's trying to solve a puzzle.

In his deep gravel voice, almost like a growl, he said, "What's that?"

"Sir?"

Long pause.

"What's that?"

I figure out he's looking at the patch of hair on my chin.

"Well, Coach, it's a goatee."

"A what?"

"A goatee."

"Why?"

"Umm, I just like it. Thought I'd try it out."

"Umm."

Long pause.

"When are you coming back?" He never did tell me to shave it.

CHAPTER FIVE

I must have been in my own head somewhere at that point because the next thing I can remember about the pregame atmosphere is Weeb walking in and scratching his scalp as he looked around the locker room. Traditionally, he talked to us after we returned from warm-ups, prior to going out to start the game. But it's all last-minute stuff by then, quick reminders on who to watch and some words to fire us up. Just like any other game day, we settled in and gave him our full attention. I patted the tape on my cleats as Coach Ewbank paced into the middle of the room wearing his rumpled gray suit.

"Gosh, guys, you have all done a heck of a job getting us here this year."

"Heck" was as close as Coach Ewbank got to swearing, but don't worry, the rest of the team did our best to make up for him.

"The offense..." he looked around and nodded to the entire room, "you guys have been good."

The defensive players all nodded and a few of the other guys clapped and hooted.

Coach walked across the room and then back to where he started. "The defense! You guys have been terrific." The offensive players, myself included, nodded and cheered in agreement. They had been the best in the league.

"Shucks, guys," Coach continued, before taking a brief pause.

It's worth noting here that with Weeb, the word "shucks" was reserved for dire circumstances or when you really messed up and he needed to express frustration. "I've got a problem here. I don't know who we should introduce, the offense or the defense, because you both have been so darned good."

By introduction, Weeb meant which eleven players would gather before the game and run out toward midfield and break out to the bench as the P.A. announced their names to the entire stadium. It was an honor, an individual recognition for the player.

There was nodding in acknowledgment of the problem— a few people were playing this straight. Somebody on the defensive team said, "Just introduce the defense."

That broke the room up, and, just like Curley's well-timed words of wisdom on the bus, bonded us closer together.

"Well, Coach," I interrupted, "just introduce the seniors." That was how they did it at college games, and that got a laugh.

Weeb started laughing and waved us all off. "Fine, I'll introduce the defense."

The entire team left the locker room as one unit, feeling loose. We were having fun. We had prepared and were confident and ready to go. We knew what we were doing so we could relax. The adrenaline pumping through our bodies was all positive.

* * *

Now, don't get me wrong. We weren't overconfident and had a lot of respect for the Baltimore Colts, who had been touted by the media as the best football squad to ever play. They had only lost one game early in the season, to Cleveland, and then got revenge by beating the Browns in the NFL Championship Game, 34–0. We had a secret weapon, though, one that the media had unintentionally helped us build and lulled the Colts to sleep with: the AFL's reputation.

The Jets, like practically every AFL team, had former NFL rejects. I was not aware of it going in the other direction. In other words, I had never heard of any pro being cut from an AFL team and picked up by an NFL organization. But there were a few players, like Matt Snell and myself, who had been drafted by both NFL and AFL teams and picked what was perceived as the lesser league. Snell was the first upset that Mr. Werblin scored for the Jets by signing him away from the New York Giants in 1964. I also picked the AFL over the NFL and had a lot of AFL pride. We were the underdogs, like back in Beaver Falls with the kids from the Lower End, and that was a powerful feeling. You want to find a way to stay hungry. Even at Alabama, where we were often the favored team, Coach Bryant always found a way to give us a sense of urgency and confidence while never allowing for a sense of overconfidence.

While I was growing up, that's the one thing I wasn't, especially when it came to my education. I attended Catholic school as a kid, and it was far more rigid than anything else in my life. I went to eight a.m. Mass at St. Mary's Grammar School every morning, and I could recite the Lord's Prayer without even thinking, like every good Catholic kid. But that wasn't where I connected to a sense of a higher power. I had to find my own way to that connection and at the time it wasn't by sitting still in a church following rules. Whenever that priest got to sermonizing, I'd get to thinking about the upcoming sandlot game with the gang a few blocks away or daydreaming about how my hero, Roberto Clemente, hit so well. I did not feel that same sense of spiritual comfort with most of the nuns at school. Most were wonderfully kind sisters, but others seemed hell-bent on abusing their power and ran classes like dictators.

In seventh grade, for example, there was a girl in class who flirted with me occasionally. She tugged my shirt once as the nun was writing on the chalkboard, and I turned around to see what was going on, and the girl made a friendly face. I didn't notice the nun staring at me. I didn't even notice her walking down the row of desks. Finally, I picked up on the angry swishing of her habit as she neared, but turned around too late. She wound up, cocked that arm like she was about to throw a fastball, and caught me across the face with the nastiest slap I ever received. Talk about a quick release. This sister had practice.

My cheek burned, both from the hit and from fury over the stinging meanness. I knew, even then, that this was not right and that sparked this explosion of emotion inside me. I didn't care that I was just a kid and that I was taught good manners and to always respect adults—this was simply not right, and I found myself incapable of just sitting there and taking it.

I stared at the nun and did not see one iota of regret in her tensed face. This was a battle of wills. It was about answering to some inner belief that was not going to allow me to accept the verdict when I knew the punishment didn't match the crime. My brothers went to St. Mary's and may have earned a rebellious reputation that carried over to me, but that's an oversimplification. What happened had nothing to do with respecting authority. My reaction was a result of somebody abusing power and belittling me. It may have just been a slap to her, one that she dished out a few times a week, but this was the first major character moment for me—how was I going to react? Sit down and apologize and take it?

I stood up, gathered up my things, and turned my back on her. The whole class was silent as I slowly walked over to the window, opened it, and threw all of my books outside. No, I wasn't disrespectful. I didn't cuss her out or have a temper tantrum. That was just my way of letting her know that she had crossed a boundary.

Of course, I did have to deal with other levels of established power at St. Mary's, but it's odd in that I can acutely remember that incident and nothing about what happened afterward. I couldn't tell you if I went to the principal's office or if I was suspended or caned with a wooden ruler. In my head, it didn't even matter. What mattered was that I stood up for myself. I had no problem facing the consequences. Even in the heat of the confrontation, I knew I wasn't going to get off without punishment and that was fine. It wasn't about getting away with something or plea-bargaining down punishment—this was all an internal decision, one where I truly felt I had no choice but to follow.

I was not asked back to St. Mary's for the eighth grade. Actually, my parents were told that I wasn't welcome back, which I was fine with for several reasons. All my friends that I palled around with, fished with, played sandlot ball with were going to Beaver Falls Junior High. Lunchtime stick-ball at St. Mary's had been fun, but my new school had a baseball, football, and basketball team. And, no more Mass every morning and slapping nuns and airborne books.

I was nervous going to the school for the first day, but it seemed most of the other students were as well. I wasn't used to such a big school, so I took a seat near the back row for my first class. The teacher walked into the room and introduced himself and began calling roll. He went down his list, shouting students' names, and they put up their hand and said, "Here, sir." He did the Ls and the Ms and when he got to the Ns he paused.

"Namath."

I put my hand up, but before I could open my mouth, he said, "Are you related to Frank Namath and Bob Namath?"

"Yes, sir. They're my—"

"Up here," he demanded, his attitude changing as he pointed with a stern finger at a desk closer to him.

"You sit here in front of me and you keep your mouth shut."

My brothers and sister were constantly complaining about how annoying I was and what a hassle it was to have a little brother tagging along. This was the first time that I had to suffer for them obviously being pains in the butt to somebody else.

My brothers had all moved out by then, however, and I missed them more than at any other time in my life. There was a sense of security from having family around, even if they showed it with a punch to the arm or a body check running down the stairs. Even when we were supposed to be sleeping, we had all sorts of games we would play. My favorite was when Frank and I shared a bed and we'd draw pictures of something in the room on each other's backs, just using our fingernail. I might sketch a lamp or clothes hanger or my cap gun. We'd get three guesses to try to figure out what the image was and if we failed, we had to scratch the other one's back fifty or a hundred times, counting out loud, depending on what we had agreed on to make sure there was no shorting.

One night, when I was four, Frank was snoring loudly beside me when I was woken up by a burst of shouting. My parents were downstairs, and the voices were clearly theirs. I listened to another loud exchange that carried with it an undercurrent of anger that scared me more than any of the imaginary ghosts lurking near the basement bathroom. I looked over to Frank, shaking him, hoping he'd wake and do something to make me feel safer, protected, in control. But he was lost in a deep teenage slumber.

Another bout of arguing came up the stairs and I became so unsettled that I couldn't stay still in bed. Nervous energy and fear made me get up and walk to the top of the stairs. I sat down on the top step, unnoticed, listening as my parents faced each other. I'd never heard them like this—two powerful emotional forces with neither one willing to give an inch. They'd never argued in English before—it was always Hungarian—never mind with this much intensity.

Dad took an angry breath and yelled, "All right, damn it, I'll leave!"

His words struck me with such sharpness that I didn't know how to handle the sting. Perhaps I intuitively understood that my parents were not happy with each other even as they loved us.

"Please don't go!" I yelled down to him, crying.

They froze, and suddenly those two formidable emotional forces that had been verbally bashing each other rushed up and both held me, and I felt a crashing wave of love.

"It's okay, Joey," my mom said and kissed my forehead.

"I'm not going anywhere," Dad said.

They stayed with me there until I calmed down. I knew they both loved me and at that moment it was enough to give me some comfort. They quietly walked me back into my room, Frank still lightly snoring, and tucked me in beside him. They both kissed me and told me how much they loved me again, before walking out of the room. Frank grunted, his snoring momentarily halted as I scooted closer and put my arm around him.

My parents did their best to keep their problems away from us kids, but my older brothers and sister had to have known what was happening. I later learned that my dad had been seeing another woman, a widow, and my mother must have found out. As a devout Catholic, divorce was very painful for her because at that time, it meant excommunication from the Church and that she wouldn't be able to receive sacraments or last rites. It must have been awful for her to agree to the divorce, which happened before I began eighth grade.

Meanwhile, Sonny and his wife Sharon were making the military their career. Rita had graduated and joined the army. Frank was at the University of Kentucky and Bob had a family and worked in a steel mill. I could tell Mom was deeply hurt and I did my best to look like I was doing all right, too, but I knew I couldn't take care of her then. I did, however, feel a more important bond with her after the divorce—it was just the two of us, and we both knew it was going to be a struggle.

We had to sell the house and move into a smaller place. Then we bounced from apartment to apartment, seemingly every few months. I liked the newfound freedom, but it wasn't perfect. We lived above a gin mill, and one day I complained to Mom that my legs were tingling at night. I would get into bed and feel this itching pins and needles. She listened and then pulled the covers on my bed back to investigate. I can still remember her scream as she watched a bed full of cockroaches scurry away from the exposure. We moved out as quickly as possible, a few days at most after that incident.

My life had been forcefully broken apart and it hurt. Dad had moved out and I wasn't even sure where he lived. Mom began working multiple jobs, and even with my limited understanding of finances at the time, I clearly recognized how tough getting by was for her. Dad had never sat me down and explained…anything really, so I was sorting through the pain of a family torn apart and the confusion over the why and how life could transform so quickly. I have learned how complicated relationships can get, and I don't want to assign blame, but I saw, daily, how difficult Mom's life was immediately after the divorce.

So, I took all those tightly packed emotions and let them unravel on the fields and courts. I wasn't an angry athlete like some people I'd play with later. I wasn't aggressively dominant to compensate for the fragility I felt at home. Instead, in sports I found a sense of control that led to a peace of mind in my daily life. Even when I made mistakes, or my team was losing, I had the ability to effect change. I grew to love and accept that sense of responsibility, and sports soon became my greatest form of therapy.

But I had to set some rules at home, too. I matured. I went from a spoiled kid in a loving home with a family to having all my siblings move out, my home sold, my parents split, and obvious financial instability for a few years. Understandably, Mom was also frustrated and once started to say something about Dad; I looked at her, and while I saw her pain and anger, I wasn't the right person for her to talk to and asked her to stop. "Don't talk about Dad, Mom." She just nodded, apologized, and gave me a hug. Unsurprisingly, an almost identical situation came up with my dad, and he reacted the same way. In an interview years later for the *New York Times,* Mom was asked how she thought the divorce had affected me. "We had a nice life while it lasted," she said. "Joe was close to his father. He still is—and I've never stood in the way."

My older brothers and sister were on their own and didn't have to interact with everybody on a consistent basis, and they clearly had different feelings about the situation that led to the breakup. But Mom got along just fine. She made me breakfast and kissed me good-bye, and I wouldn't see her until she got off work at night and we had dinner together. She worked most weekends, and I went from a somewhat spoiled kid to an almost Huckleberry Finn lifestyle. There were hardly any restrictions now that my brothers and sister had left and Dad wasn't living with us. Mom might get a swat in if I crossed the line, but, generally speaking, Dad had been the disciplinarian in the family.

While it wasn't too common, he would sometimes take me to the coal cellar to dish out serious whuppings.

Still, I almost always listened to Mom and respected her, but c'mon, I was way faster than her. No way was she going to be able to catch me. Maybe dodging and juking Mom is one reason I did okay on the field? I'd had practice in the home since I was a toddler. I'd see her face flash with anger and even though I might be next to her, she'd swat at me or try to smack my bottom and I always cut left or right and could accelerate past her until she finally started chuckling. Another time when I was around fifteen, I rubbed her the wrong way and she told me to get out of the kitchen. I can't remember why, but I started laughing. She looked down at the table and picked up an apple and threw it at me. Even though I was only ten feet away, I could duck it easily. I had some nervous laughing now when she picked up a cup and threw it. I managed to avoid that projectile, too, but when she picked up the fork, I paid a little more attention and bobbed and weaved to make her miss. I made a prudent decision after that and got out the door, onto the street, and good-bye.

No running from Dad, though—that would have only made things worse. I'd take that solemn walk down to the cellar and into the coal room. But, too soon, the cellar and Dad's involvement were a thing of the past.

I may have charmed myself out of some situations, but I do feel that I've always been willing to face the consequences of my actions when I've done something wrong. And I've had to do that plenty. When I know my hands are clean, though, I will push back against anything I see as unfair.

And, in 1968, what felt like an unfair feeling was broadcast wide by media, by fans, by NFL coaches and players once they knew the Jets had made it to the Championship Game. It only felt natural for me to offer some resistance. Atlanta Falcons coach and former NFL quarterback Norm Van Brocklin was asked for his assessment of me as a quarterback before the 1968 Super Bowl and couldn't help but take a shot at the AFL: "I'll tell you what I think about Joe Namath on Sunday night—after he has played his first pro game."

You always got taunts and trash talk—heck, they should have given Johnny Sample an award for that at the Touchdown Club that infamous night I gave the guarantee—but I had experienced our league's disrespect straight from a Colts player's mouth.

* * *

A few nights before the big game, Lou Michaels (the Colts defensive tackle and kicker) and Dan Sullivan (an offensive guard) met me and Jim Hudson (our strong safety from the University of Texas) for dinner at Frankie's, an Italian spot on US 1. It was a nice joint. The waiters wore jackets, and I had on some tailored shirt—one that hadn't been ruined by the dry cleaners yet—from a little place on First Avenue in the city that did my clothes. I had known Michaels from way back because my brother Frank had gone to Kentucky with him. He was a year ahead of my brother, but since he was from Pennsylvania, too, they just hit it off. When I was in junior high, they'd driven up from Kentucky, and I had gotten to meet Lou, who was an All-American lineman and an exciting guy to shake hands with.

Anyway, we were drinking at Frankie's bar. I was sipping a Scotch on the rocks with Jim when Lou and Dan strolled in. There was respect there. I liked Lou. He was older than me and certainly had seniority. Hud and I were only in our fourth year in the pros.

But get this. After some small talk, Lou, who was a big guy with a square jaw and all, leans in and says, "Joe, you know we're going to kick your ass."

I just laughed at him. It was ridiculous! I looked at him and said, "C'mon, man, not now!" We were about to sit down for a nice meal. "C'mon."

He stared at me. "I'm going to tell you why. We're going to bring in Johnny [Unitas] and Johnny is going to get it done."

In the meantime, they had Earl Morrall, the MVP of the NFL, as their quarterback. Johnny U was an amazing player, but he was injured. It wasn't meant with any disrespect, but I had to bust chops with Lou.

"Aw, come on, Lou, what are you talking about? And besides, what do you know about it? You're just a damn kicker." He didn't like that. Not a bit. But I decided to keep going. "Johnny is hurt. He's been hurt all year—he can't throw a ball across the street."

Lou straightened up and leaned that big jaw of his into my face. I thought, "Uh-oh…" And by the grace of God, one of the hosts felt the heat. He quickly came over and nervously got between us. "Hey, hey, let's calm down!"

I believe this gentleman may have saved my life. Or he could have also just wanted to save his bar from the ensuing tussle. Lou, though, he really thought his Colts were going to kick our asses, and that was telling. Even so, we all sat down, I had a nice piece of meat, and it was a great meal together. Lou and Sullivan played for the opposing team, but they were good company and it was the last we talked about the game.

Weeb, however, wanted to see me the next day before practice. The afternoon was oppressively hot and I might have been taking a tad longer to tape up, still shaking some fuzz off from some extracurricular activities the night before. I had a sense Weeb was upset because word had gotten around about me saying something about a guarantee when Frank Ramos, our media director, was with me at the award dinner.

The headline about the guarantee had been printed in the newspaper, so there had been a lot of stuff going around when Weeb called me into the center of the field with offensive coordinator Clive Rush. Clive was our wideout and backfield coach—we only had four coaches beside Weeb. There wasn't the type of payroll they can afford today.

I went out there and could tell…I could sense I was about to get yelled at as I saw Weeb in that beautiful Florida air, arms folded as he watched me jogging toward him. When a player is called over to a coach, you get over on the double. The cuffs on his slacks were rolled up to keep them clean, and his black shoes and white laces were visible from across the field. Even though it was January and was hot, he wore his standard Jets-green windbreaker. Clive towered over Weeb wearing his Jets jacket, too.

There was a feeling inside me, man—it was the same one I had always gotten when Dad took me down to the basement with the strap as a kid. You know, Weeb had this way of standing when he was negotiating a contract or about to say something firm—he'd cross his arms, tight as possible, and just hold them there until the storm had blown over. When you saw that body language, the way he braced, then you knew that Weeb wasn't going to budge.

I wasn't too worried, though. Growing up, I had a lot of practice charming myself out of situations. If I was bored at school, which was often, sitting behind a desk was borderline torture for me. Impossible even. I'd find a pencil and I'd draw on my books. Once, just before Mrs. Berard's typing class started, I was horsing around with a Zippo lighter at my desk. There's a way you can pop the lid and strike a flame in one motion, and I was practicing it. Mesmerized, I didn't pay attention to the girl sitting in front of me, and when she leaned back the flame instantly curled her hair black before shooting up the back of her head. Instantly, I started smacking her hair trying to put it out. She turned to see what the heck was going on and started swatting at the flames herself. We were all terrified, frightened by the terrible smell more than anything else. Mrs. Berard came over and was understanding when I explained the accident and luckily didn't administer any punishment. My daughters were damn near incredulous when I told them the story the first time. Apparently lighters are frowned upon in school these days.

Even years before when I wasn't horsing around at school, me and Linwood would sometimes sneak over to the massive junkyard near our house. It seemed like the fenced-in area went on for a few football fields, filled with rusted-out junkers, big metal pipes, a metal boat with a hole in it, and literally tons of little odds and ends. We'd usually wait until dark and then dig out some of the dirt under the fence and crawl through. Our shirts had long marks of filth from crawling, but back then most kids wore hand-me-downs anyway—pants with patches, shoes with holes in them, that kind of thing. Kids were expected to get dirty. When we didn't hear anybody coming, we'd spend half an hour or so digging around through the scraps, finding little odd things that looked valuable. We stashed them behind Linwood's house and in the morning walked over and sold them back to the junkyard owner, Mr. Shansky, for pennies and nickels. Looking back, I really do believe that he knew what we were doing and was a good sport about it.

For some reason we didn't consider that stealing, though. We would never break into a house or take somebody's purse, but we thought of our taking empty bottles off back porches and junkyard recycling more as hustling. And if anybody disagreed with our rationale, well, that was when I worked that charm.

* * *

I jogged up close to Weeb and played it sweet.

"Hey, Coach."

He shot back, "What have you done?!" in the slightly high-pitched voice he used when upset. "Do you know what you've done? Do you know what you've done?!" I stood there, arms down, palms up, face confused.

"No, Coach. What have I done?"

Weeb was serious and upset. I had respect for him and he never really got like this unless it was for a good reason. And, by the way, I knew he was right.

I respected my coaches. Coach Bryant was big on respect—to everybody. In 1984, they did a movie on him called *The Bear,* and there was a scene in which a doctor introduced himself to Coach and put his hand out, and in the scene Coach Bryant didn't shake hands with him. In fact, the Coach Bryant character made it a point not to put his hand out.

That was it for me right there—I had to stop watching. Coach Bryant was tough, boy, but he respected other people, and the depiction just didn't seem right or honest. Clearly, they were trying to show a certain hardness about him. But they got it wrong. Coach Bryant was a gentleman and respected everybody that I ever saw him with. That is unless you didn't own up. Now, if you lied to him, if you didn't keep your word, if you cut four classes, Coach Bryant would look at you differently, if not worse. You could cut three classes if you had an excuse. But that fourth one— you had to sit with Coach Bryant in his office, and tell him why you cut, and then go out and run with another coach at six in the morning. They'd literally run you into the ground, man. Players would collapse and vomit. Considering that, I was too scared to cut more than three.

Anyway, I stood on the practice field before the Super Bowl game and watched Weeb's arms tighten across his chest even more, pulling down his coach's whistle as he looked up at me under the bill of his Jets ball cap.

"You know what you have done?!" he said again. "Coach Shula is going to take these newspaper clippings and tack them up on the bulletin board in the locker room, and the first thing those players are going to see when they come in is those darn quotes, and they're going to get fired up."

I assumed he was right. Actually, Weeb had coached Shula in the 1950s, and now they were going against each other in the Super Bowl. Two future Hall of Fame coaches. The best coaches have a way of operating off a strong foundation of respect, a notion that I believe is a secret to success not only in football, but also in life. I loved Coach Bryant even more when I saw how he treated his players' parents.

Don Shula is also a man I respect and learned from. The first year I was doing some color work, for NBC, the Miami

Dolphins were one of the games I covered. Shula was now the head coach and I took my dad down to one of their practices. Shula had been the Baltimore Colts head coach, you know, but that didn't matter in his world regarding how he treated people. Coach Shula just made my dad feel so good, started speaking Hungarian to him. Two Hungarians. Yeah, they just started talking Hungarian. It tickled me, and my dad got a kick out of that. That was good. But back in 1969, I wasn't sure how Coach Shula—even though the Colts team was a reflection of him and didn't play dirty—was going to react to my guarantee of a win.

Anyway, Coach Ewbank kept his arms folded through all of this, braced, and I was already in my "Aw, shucks" posture as I said, "But, Coach," making my eyes as puppy dog as possible, "it's your fault."

That one finally broke his composure and his firm face went from squinted eye to genuine confusion.

"What?"

"You told us. You said we were going to win the game. You're the one giving us confidence. You've been there before. You've won championships."

Heck, Weeb had won an NFL Championship coaching the Baltimore Colts. He was the one who had brought in Johnny U, my childhood hero. He had proven that he knew how to get it done, so I figured, why not just say what the whole team thought: We were going to win.

I was really dipping my head by now though, in full bad dog pose, playing it up as he unfolded his arms and waved me off in exasperation. I couldn't hide my grin by that point and he knew I was pulling his leg. "Get out of here! Get…get out of here!"

Well, I took off, running across that field, chuckling to myself. Obviously, it was never meant to give anybody any extra motivation, but the reality was that after analyzing things, knowing how I reacted on championship teams, knowing my own physiology—when you are a favorite, when you are supposed to win, when you are continually told how good you are, it has an effect. And the Colts were told, rightfully so, how good they were throughout the entire season. They proved it.

The execution of their defense was unparalleled. It was awesome. Bubba Smith was six-foot-seven and ran like a gazelle. I can state with authority that as a player coming at you, he was factually a quarterback's worst nightmare. Just sensational.

The Colts were overconfident, even if they would never admit such a thing. Meanwhile, we had to beat the Oakland Raiders to win the AFL Championship, and it was one of the toughest, most physical games I had ever played in and still came out a winner. Usually, when you take a physical beating like that, you lose. Oakland was real good, but certainly had some players who completely disregarded the rules of decent sportsmanship. Ben Davidson, known as Gentle Ben, was also around six-foot-seven, and during one of our first games he hit me late. He jammed his elbow into my gut while on top and pushed off my head to get up, smooshing my face into the muddy field. He had also once stuck his hand under my mask and clawed his fingers down my face. After unsticking my helmet from the mud and watching him walk away, I ran up and grabbed him from behind and said something I'm not proud of to this day. But I had to let him know he couldn't get away with that again. He had crossed the line. It was flat-out dirty. Those games against Oakland were hell, but it was a special kind of anticipation going into them because you knew how sore you were going to be the next morning, win or lose.

Weeb was not a conspiracy theorist, but he did think the Raiders had people spying on our practices and he would get a funny look when a helicopter flew over the field. Al Davis, Oakland's owner, was known around the league as an overaggressive competitor who would bend the rules as far as possible to ensure a positive outcome for his team. There were further accusations of creating a soggy field and letting the grass grow longer to slow our team down, which was much faster than the Raiders. And I do have to admit that we came out of those games a little extra muddy.

The Jets were a respectable team and had a fine reputation, like the Colts in the NFL, but the Raiders lapped up that negative Bad Boy attention and fed the press quote after quote. But I was pretty good at giving it back. When I'd be particularly beat-up after a game, I'd straighten up around the reporters and smile as if I were coming out of a day spa. One of the Raiders broke my cheekbone during a game, and when asked by the press about it, I replied that I had a particularly tough steak at the pregame meal. I might be asked about a certain dirty hit and I'd shrug, almost as if I wasn't sure what they were talking about and mention that I've been beat up more by my sister, Rita. It would work, too. The next day or so we'd see some quote from a Raiders player outright saying we were asking for it.

For that AFL Championship Game, though, there was a hit that required smelling salts to bring me back. By today's standards, I would have been pulled from the field following concussion protocol. I wouldn't have been allowed back in the game. There were tackles when Oakland would get you down and just keep piling on. And let me tell you—they do fall on you on purpose. Absolutely! Putting my hand up to keep an Oakland player off me caused a dislocated middle finger. I ran to the sidelines and held my hand out, not looking as our trainer popped it back into place, taped it to a good finger, and sent me back out onto the field. But those little reminders were Oakland's calling card, and it's no secret that they were known for playing…well, dirty.

Considering all that, you can imagine how much craziness and celebrating there was after the win against the Raiders to secure a place in the Super Bowl. There were champagne bottles popping and squirting foam at each other amid dancing and hoots and cheering. The fact that we had to beat the Raiders, our fiercest AFL rival and a team we felt sometimes pushed the limits of sportsmanship, made it that much sweeter.

So, *beating* the Raiders was enjoyable and usually hard to accomplish. We enjoyed beating them. We wanted to win against the Colts, but we wanted to beat the Raiders. That AFL win was where we really cut loose and exhaled after a season that started so shaky.

Again, my two goals going all the way back to Little League had always been to first make the team and then win the championship. That hadn't changed as a professional. I now had the opportunity to achieve that at the highest level with the upcoming World Championship Game.

CHAPTER SIX

Looking at the screen, I am still only on the Super Bowl warm-ups when I pause the game to consider how well my memory is aligning with what I see on the tape. This ability to recollect, well, I don't think it's so clear cut. I mean, there's a general saying in sports that "the most important game is the next one on the schedule," and we all subscribed to that. Our Jets celebrated after a victory, but then we knew it was behind us. We were on to the next season, new wins and losses. In the mental archive I keep of all the games I've played in my career, what happened on the field during the Super Bowl has been filed alongside all the others in my mind.

And like any other regular season game I might get asked about, I need to dig to remember the plays and events for our championship wins as well. With the help of hyperbaric oxygen therapy, I still have mental access to many of my past experiences. But I do find it amazing how much more vivid those memories are of the losses and miscues—of the bad footwork that made a pass go off the mark, of the missed reads that led to an interception or the open receiver I didn't spot in time—than the victories and good plays. More than that, it's always my contributions to the loss that are front and center, waving their hands and shouting for me to give them some more attention.

I decide that I should get my heart rate up, so I head over to the NordicTrack to get my workout in like I have for the past forty-one years. If you have bum knees, you can't do better than this zero-impact machine. I get on, my mind starts wandering, and not three minutes in, the damn 1963 Auburn game starts clawing its way into my thoughts— the game where I overthrew Benny Nelson. Most athletes, whether they're in the Hall of Fame or only played JV ball, come back to certain plays during a bout of daydreaming, which I often do while exercising. At some moment during my workout, that quarterback sneak I ran against Jim Hudson's Texas team in the 1965 Orange Bowl will always come drifting into mental view.

Kansas City in the 1969 AFL semifinals, too. I think about that a lot. Bobby Bell made a fantastic play. In fact, we laughed about it years later when he brought it up. Well, he laughed and I grumbled. It still stung. Bobby had been disciplined and stayed with Snell, his assignment on our right flat, and he never went for the inside fake I was hoping he'd go for. I had to eat the ball, we had to go for a field goal, and our team ended up losing 13–6.

There's a certain bond between players who spend so many seasons trying to outwit each other, and at least in my opinion, it's based on a lot of respect. It can become an individual chess match with Bell and players like Washington's safety Kenny Houston or the Miami Dolphins defensive stars Jake Scott and Nick Buoniconti. Very smart guys who are all Hall of Famers. They were always giving me phony defensive looks and fake first steps.

Sometimes that NordicTrack makes me feel like some Charles Dickens character being haunted by the Ghosts of Games Past. So, oddly, I mentally register, as I get off and wipe the sweat from my forehead, how excited I am to spend energy remembering a game that I won.

I drink some of my vinegar water, settle into my kitchen chair again, and start the video.

* * *

What we had to accomplish as a team, all the trust we needed to have in each other, came bubbling up as I watched the camera pan around the field on my computer screen. Hud and I were close so we'd walked out together as the team took the field. Helmets on, we began strolling into the end zone. The marching band seemed to be blowing and beating their instruments extra hard and the level of crowd noise on the field was disorienting, but nothing I hadn't experienced at Alabama. I looked over at Hudson, whose face showed the same level of joy as we both cracked smiles.

We slowed slightly and looked around at the stadium, feeling another level of energy with almost seventy-five thousand people already whipped up into a frenzy. We were grinning ear to ear and I was grateful to have a good friend there to share my feelings with as I felt my focus and adrenaline begin to pump into that game zone.

"Hey, Hud,"—I leaned into Hudson's ear so he could hear me—"this is our kind of game."

"We've been here before," he shot back. Four years

earlier in the Orange Bowl, Hudson and I had walked out onto this same field to a full stadium as millions more watched the game on television. That night, I also saw Hudson line up, but for the other team. That was January 1965 and the Longhorns were playing our Crimson Tide. Hudson had come in as a substitute quarterback and nailed George Sauer with a sixty-nine-yard touchdown pass. We lost to Texas 21–17 and, man, did that ever hurt. That's another game that regularly haunts me. I never even heard that the writers had awarded me the Most Valuable Player until they sent the trophy to my house. The statue did little to erase the dull emotional smothering that comes from a big loss.

And now here we were, four years later, me glancing over to Sauer, holding his helmet in his hands as he looked up at the cloudy sky that was dark enough they'd already started warming up the lights. John Elliott, our defensive tackle, and Pete Lammons, our tight end, were in that Orange Bowl game, too. Paul Crane was also linebacker and center on the Crimson Tide. Having battled them before on this same field, I'd witnessed firsthand how gritty, tough, and talented these players were.

I was sure thankful they were wearing Jets uniforms as I went to the 50-yard line for the coin toss. Watching that moment now, you can see the ref coming over to us as he calls the captains. There isn't much I can drum up about the emotions pulsing through me at that moment, but I do remember looking across the field and seeing Johnny Unitas and it was just, "Whoa! Look where we are, man. This is it. The big one." In fact, the only time I had the opportunity to pick a number for my jersey was during my senior year in high school. I decided on Johnny's number 19. And I even got called "Joey U" a time or two.

Unitas was a decade older than me, and I'd grown up idolizing the guy and drawing on his competitive spirit while playing in high school. He had tried out for the Steelers and they let him go. Who grabbed him as quickly as possible? Our leader, Weeb Ewbank, when he was coaching the NFL Colts before he was fired and came over to the AFL Jets. Both of those guys knew something about competitive spirit.

My competitive drive against my brother Frank might have been just as intense. The first time I can remember beating him in anything was when I was around six and we were playing a small pinball-like baseball game with tin walls around the outfield to keep the toy ball in play. It's tiny, and you have a spring bat, and the other player "pitches" to you, and you have a spring to wind up your swing on the back of the machine. Frank always smoked me in this game. But on one pitch I let go a little earlier than usual, and it knocked a home run over the left field wall and I won the game. Frank took that one loss, but I could tell he was miffed. But that one win for me meant so much and helped me pursue and chase down the little victories that gave me the confidence to become a better athlete.

Growing up, I used to always imagine somebody was watching me when I was playing alone, even though the only opponent I had was my imagination. Not out of ego— the exact opposite. I wanted the pressure to perform. I used to take a golf ball—because they bounce so fast and unpredictably—and throw it against a wall so it would bounce faster and faster and try and catch it. And, as I did that, I imagined my brothers or sister watching. This drill helped me develop hand and eye speed as well as footwork coordination.

At Alabama, that became a reality for every player, with Coach Bryant up in his tower. One flick of a glance and you'd be on his radar, and he'd better see you giving it your all. And Coach had a brutal way of practicing that took some getting used to. They used to call it "getting run off" when you couldn't take it anymore and quit college and went home.

My freshman year, I went through two roommates. Fast. The first was a teammate from Rhode Island, and he lasted maybe a month, a few weeks. My second also made it for about a month, before heading back to Memphis. It's always hard being away from home for the first time, but as a football player, it felt extra rough. The practices were incredibly strenuous. But my Rhode Island roommate exemplified another tricky part of playing for Alabama: navigating all the accents. Boy, did I have a tough time understanding the Southern dialect—those guys talkin' with a pace that could beat molasses to dryin' and draggin' their vowels so long I'd forget what the word was. Meanwhile, my Rhode Island roommate talked so fast I could barely understand him! That was nothing, though—I had much bigger communication problems with Coach Bryant.

Early in August one day after high school we had an unexpected visitor show up at our doorstep in Beaver Falls, unannounced. It turned out his name was coach Howard Schnellenberger, and he was the tight end and wide receiver coach for the University of Alabama. My mother, Howard, and I sat in the front room and talked for not even an hour. That's how long it took Mom to take a liking to him before she disappeared upstairs. She brought down a small green suitcase, already packed with my clothes. She handed me a five-dollar bill and said: "Honey, you're going with him."

Man, she wanted me out of the house.

When we arrived in Tuscaloosa, Coach Schnellenberger told me we were going to meet Coach Bryant. We parked and walked across the blacktop and through the gate as I took in the fields where the team was practicing. I had changed my clothes before Mom sent me on my way, and I was wearing my favorite hat—a powder-blue straw number with a pearl pin in the hatband.

Coach Bryant glanced down from his tower, around two stories high. I stared, amazed—and instantly realized what a difference college football was from high school. Players were separated into offense, running plays, and others were going through defensive exercises. There were so many players doing so many different things that I needed a moment to take it all in. When I looked back up to that tower I saw that Coach Bryant had his eyes on everyone, slowly scanning, watching and analyzing every move of every player.

We walked along the sidelines. Coach Bryant made eye contact with Schnellenberger and when we got close enough, they started talking. I swear their accents were so drawn out that they might as well have been talking in code. I had no idea what the conversation was about so I just focused on watching the drills.

"Coach Bryant wants to see you."

Now that I understood. I looked up.

As a kid, I had shimmied up exterior pipe to retrieve our balls from the roof of the abandoned laundromat, so I had no problem ascending the ladder that led up to that tower. I stuck my head through the opening in the floor. Coach Bryant saw me and nodded to come up. I introduced myself. I didn't know then that I had entered hallowed ground. It wasn't until later I was told Coach rarely invited anyone to his perch. At that point, though, I was just excited to meet my new coach.

He greeted me and started to talk as he invited me to look out at my new teammates. Again, I ran into a translation problem as he began talking with that Southern accent. No disrespect intended, but to me it sounded like grumbling with a growl thrown in for punctuation. Literally, the only word I understood was "stud." I think he said something about Alabama and pointed to a player below him running drills: "Stud!"

He'd point to another player who just caught a pass and grumble something, and the only word I'd pick out again was "Stud!" I picked up what it meant to be a stud, and it was obvious that I was about to be surrounded by a bunch of them.

I just kept nodding respectfully. I was up there for about five minutes, nodding and saying "Yes, sir." Then we shook hands and I descended from the perch, back to earth again. We immediately left practice for the Greyhound bus station. NCAA rules asserted that Alabama couldn't fly me in to enroll in school, but flights were permissible for a recruiting visit. Then the recruit had to leave town. Technically my flight with Coach Schnellenberger was my official visit to the school and now I was driven to the

Greyhound bus station to get out of town and find my way back to Tuscaloosa to enroll. I was told to look for a tall gentleman in a suit at the station and his name, in all seriousness, was Mr. Lackey.

"He'll pick you up and make it all happen smoothly," Coach said as he dropped me off and handed me my bus ticket to Birmingham. Man, had it turned into a very strange twenty-four hours. I had gone from expecting to maybe hang with Linwood or shoot some pool that night to being flown out of Beaver Falls and into Alabama and taken onto a football field, invited up into Coach Bryant's tower and then, like some spy movie, sent off on a bus to meet a stranger.

I said good-bye and walked to a bench to wait for my bus. I was feeling excited about what I'd seen and my future at Alabama, but then I looked up. That indigestible pit came back into my stomach as I saw the water fountains against the wall by the bathrooms: one for white and one for colored. I tried to shake the feeling, but just couldn't. The bus came and I grabbed my suitcase and walked on, going all the way to the back. It was natural—I always went to the back of the bus. In my world, that's where all the fun happened. But in the South, I learned it was yet another way to separate people. I didn't know the back of the bus was where black people were supposed to sit. I didn't even notice the whole bus ride, until I was informed when I got off by an older white lady that I had been sitting in the "wrong" seat.

Mr. Lackey met me and I got a return ticket back to Tuscaloosa to enroll in the University of Alabama all on my own. As if to test my decision, on that trip, as the bus drove through the town of Holt, I noticed a fire in a field. My face was plastered to the window as I looked at this big burning cross with around twenty Klansmen in their white cloaks and hoods. Oh man…this is real, I thought. It had been a steady escalation from the separate drinking fountains, the bus seating, and now the burning cross and Klansmen.

Something about Coach Bryant, though, and that practice, made me want to be a part of it. The desire to be on his team overrode my differences with the South. One of the counselors picked me up at the bus station and I was given a room at the athletic dorm, Friedman Hall. My roommate—Thomas Tibedeau, a lineman—was already situated, but a few weeks later, I returned from practice to find the room cleaned out. He left without even saying good-bye.

For me, though, right away at Alabama practices felt just like they did at home when Frank was watching me. I imagined him watching me. Full speed ahead. Almost constantly active. We did very little standing around on the field. Every single one of us, coaches included, felt like Coach Bryant was watching you.

As freshmen, we were on the field farthest from Coach's tower. We didn't practice with varsity unless they wanted somebody to beat up. You knew the man was up there, and that was great. He was looking around. Every now and then Coach Bryant would say something that most everyone understood. I didn't always hear him or comprehend what he said, but stuff was going on, and I'd just jump in. The practice field was my favorite place. I was a Yankee from up north. Some of the Southerners busted my chops, but we all earned one another's respect on that turf.

And my parents had a heckuva work ethic that carried over onto the field, and I think Coach Bryant picked up on that. I even had a job every summer I had the chance. I caddied at the local country club and worked at Gus's High Hat, shining shoes. I did things to try and make money. We all did at home. Getting pop bottles, whether it was taking them off of somebody's porch, or digging through trash, but getting two cents, or selling metal we'd fished out of the river.

You just did what you had to do. You just practiced hard and played hard. That was something I learned from my high school coach, who was great too, man. Coach Larry Bruno had played football and basketball at nearby East Liverpool High in Ohio and played football at Geneva College. (Let me add that Lou Holtz, another former coach and friend who I had the honor of playing for, was also from East Liverpool, Ohio. Two great coaches from one small town.) Coach Bruno was a running back and was selected to play in the 1947 College All-Star East–West Shrine Game in San Francisco. He was also picked in the 13th round of the NFL draft by the Pittsburgh Steelers but instead pursued a career as a high school coach. He was the head football coach at Monaca, six miles south of Beaver Falls, from 1949 to '58, and Beaver Falls from 1959 to '78.

Coach Bruno was a perfectionist who stressed organization; he was an amateur magician, too, which made sense because he was an innovator when it came to designing plays that relied on timing and misdirection. Sleight of hand was his forte. One time I had faked a handoff to our fullback, Bert Kerstetter, who sold it so well that the ref thought he had the ball. Burt got tackled going into the line of scrimmage and the ref stopped play, but I was running with the ball and ran for a touchdown. I was there by myself in the end zone waving the ball at everybody.

Coach Bruno helped me more than any coach I'd had up to that time—and maybe more than any coach I ever had when it came to dealing with the specifics of the game and getting from Point A to Point B, learning footwork, and becoming the leader I needed to be as a quarterback. He was a wonderful teacher, a wonderful coach, a wonderful person. He was humble, and absolutely instrumental in getting football scholarships for so many players over the years. It was beautiful what he did for his players. I believe everybody who played under Coach Bruno came out a better person for it. And—yes, sir—every play in practice was full speed ahead.

No matter how hard I tried in high school, though, the guy in front of me, senior Richie Niedbala was better in every imaginable way. Richie and I played together as children in all the sports—Little League, Pony League, Junior Legion, and high school baseball, football, basketball. Richie was gifted. He had terrific footwork. He was a three-sport star at Beaver Falls. Richie eventually got a football scholarship to the University of Miami and later became one of the most successful high school head football coaches in western Pennsylvania.

When I did start my junior year, we had some fumbles and I had ball handling problems. Basically, I played poorly. I could still run, but Coach Bruno put in the better player. I studied Richie, admiring his competitive spirit. He had poise no matter what sport he was playing. Richie was straight-out better than me and he wasn't giving up that job. I was still learning.

Despite Richie's outstanding talent, though, I think Coach Bruno was looking ahead to build my confidence, so he started me in our final game of the season my junior year against New Brighton. We won by something like forty points, which was when everyone started to build really high hopes for our senior year. Their optimism was certainly not misdirected; that team is *still* talked about in Beaver Falls today.

* * *

I had a growth spurt that season, both mentally and physically. I went from being five-eight to six-one and it was wonderful. Fortunately it didn't affect my coordination. You see, Coach Bruno was also a choreographer who broke down every move into a sequence of steps. He coached that time matters, and he talked in split seconds. He himself was still agile, and I mimicked his movements as he demonstrated how to explode and get away from center heading in the correct direction. Coach Bruno's teachings on footwork stayed with me all through college and the pros, and I consistently taught it in my kids' football camps for forty-six years.

So, after Richie graduated, I was eager to try and prove myself. Our first game was against Midland High School, and we were anticipating a tough matchup.

The first play of the game we ran our fullback off left tackle, gained maybe two yards, but were flagged. As quarterback, I went over to the referee to see what the penalty was for, and he let me know it was on us: illegal procedure (when an offensive player moves forward before the snap of the ball). But the Midland captain accepted the penalty, which gave us the opportunity to repeat first down.

Why would you take a penalty and give us another play? Why not make it a long second down? I looked at the Midland captain and told him they'd just made a mistake. The next play we ran an option left and I stuck the ball in the belly of our fullback, Bert Kerstetter. Truth was, it was a fake and I kept the ball. Many people think a quarterback is the most important player on a fake, but I'll tell you it is the running back who has to sell the fact that he has the ball. Bert was perfect, and the Midland defense jumped all over him. As they did I took off, running left, and went sixty yards for a touchdown. Basically the same play that had fooled the ref before. We beat them by forty points.

We only had one close game that whole season. The offense we had, boy, it was wonderful and deceptive and our defense was also of championship caliber. There were a dozen guys from that team who got scholarships to play in college. On any high school team you'd be lucky to have two or three guys get offers. But that year?! It was just unbelievable. Some of us went to Division I schools and others went to smaller programs, but player after player caught the eye of one coach or another. And the guys who didn't get offers early? Coach Bruno was on the phone calling various colleges, saying to their football coaches, "This kid is a good student and he can play. Won't you give him a chance?"

We won the Western Pennsylvania Interscholastic Athletic League title that year. After that victory, a couple of us players climbed a fire escape to the roof of the Chevrolet dealership on Seventh Avenue, the main street through downtown. The business had a big helium balloon on its roof. Our plan was to paint "Take 'em Tigers" on the balloon and carry it to the school. Well, the next thing we knew we were surrounded by police, who knew us all. Heck, they had probably watched the game we were celebrating. Beaver Falls was a small town and the police were just as into sports as anybody else. Another time, a confrontation in the poolroom made its way into the alley. I was fighting this guy and the police came in with sirens and lights on. I didn't run, and the officer gets out of the car and looks at me. "Namath! What are you doing? What's wrong with you? You've got a game tomorrow. You're liable to hurt your hand. Get out of here!"

I didn't realize it at the time, but I learned so much about leadership as a high school quarterback under Coach Bruno. When you are the quarterback and step into the huddle, your demeanor is very important. Coach Bruno was all about clarity. You have to be totally focused on what you're doing on the field. We all knew and respected what he had accomplished as a player. I looked forward to every practice with him, even when the rains turned the dirt into a mud pit and we were slipping everywhere. He was talking about timing and didn't want to hear any excuses, puddles or not. Simple things, like calling a play in the huddle, speaking clearly and loud enough, and getting the play call across to everybody without having to say it more than twice, were important. It's the quarterback's job to make sure everyone understands the play and where they need to be on the field. Being accountable was important. Through watching football and learning about it from my brothers, I felt comfortable playing the position.

For all the smarts he instilled in me on the field, I wish I could say that Coach Bruno had stopped me from making stupid decisions off it, but I seemed determined to make those more than once. This might be due to the Gemini personality. I'm not sure, but I'll blame my mischief on it anyway. The first time I overdid alcohol was on my way to the annual senior school picnic; I was a late bloomer when it came to drinking. A couple of buddies and I drove the thirty-six miles from Beaver Falls to Youngstown, Ohio, where the gathering was, and we stopped at the store before we left and bought some cheap wine. I was in the backseat with the bottle and had a few sips. "Damn, I could drink this whole bottle," I said. Immediately, my buddies bet me a dollar I couldn't. Well, I won that dollar—but I wasn't in any shape to collect or spend my earnings. The next thing I remember, I was sitting at a shoeshine stand in the bathroom at an amusement park. I don't know how I got into that seat. I also can't remember how I got out of it and in the backseat of the car again for the ride home. For all the alcohol I had in the decades after that, I never had another drink of that particular brand of wine, but I damn sure won't ever forget the name: Golden Spur.

* * *

My first college campus visit was to Arizona State, in December, and then Miami after that. Before those trips, palm trees were just something mythical that existed in movies. I ended up visiting Minnesota, Michigan State, Indiana, Notre Dame, and Maryland, too. Whatever my options, I knew that when I went to college I would be headed out of Pennsylvania; I simply had no idea what the world was like elsewhere. As a family, we didn't travel far from home, nearby Massillon and Canton in Ohio to visit relatives, to Kentucky to take Frank to college, and once to Doylestown, in eastern Pennsylvania, for a baseball game. I knew my world was about to get larger, but I wasn't quite ready for anything too different just yet. I loved the weather in south Florida, and Notre Dame seemed like a great place for a kid from a strict Catholic family, but in my mind, there was only one serious contender.

I wanted to play college football at the University of Maryland because I felt comfortable with the people there, including Al Hassan, who we all called Hatchet. Al got that nickname as a little kid because his nose looked like a hatchet. Seriously.

I met Hatchet my senior year in high school, during my campus visit to College Park, Maryland. He was from New Castle, Pennsylvania, near Beaver Falls, and after a stint in the navy following high school, he attended Maryland on a scholarship as the football team's equipment manager. Hatchet was eight or nine years older, and had heard about me from his friends back home, so he was excited about me going there as well. We quickly became friends during my visit. That's also where I met my dear friend Marty Schottenheimer, also a western Pennsylvania guy, and also being recruited by Maryland. In fact, there were a number of guys from my home area, and we all met up at Maryland during our visit. To me, it was the perfect school: the campus was beautiful, Washington, DC, was right down the road, College Park was less than three hundred miles from home, plus, Tom Nugent was the head coach. He had come from Florida State, where he was successful, and had developed the I-formation when he coached at the Virginia Military Institute in 1950. I also liked that Nugent believed in the passing game.

There was just one small obstacle to overcome before I could enroll, however. In order to get into Maryland, I had to score a 750 on the College Board SAT. The first time I took the test, I didn't score high enough. Hatchet and I spent a lot of time "studying" together that summer (though I'll admit more than one of our evenings preparing for the test involved beer and a pool hall), and the university let me take the SAT a second time. My score did improve, but not by enough. I barely missed the mark. Hatchet actually saw the scores before I did and telephoned to tell me the bad news. If I couldn't get into the school, I couldn't play football for them.

I wasn't really all that upset because I thought now this meant I had no other option but to try to play professional baseball with the Cubs.

However, Coach Nugent called Coach Bryant at Alabama and told Coach Bryant that I was still available. Coach Bryant had actually sent assistant coaches Charlie Bradshaw and Dude Hennessey to Beaver Falls during basketball season to meet me, but I wasn't interested in going to Alabama at that time. Besides, they talked in such a strong Southern drawl that I really didn't understand much of what they said. I was also dead-set on Maryland, so I never made the campus visit to Tuscaloosa. But now, things had changed. It was late in the summer of 1961, I hadn't gotten into Maryland, classes were about to start, and I didn't really know what my next step was or what my future held. But I did know if I didn't go somewhere, my mother's heart would break.

So off to Alabama I went, where my freshman year almost brought me to my knees. Summer was brutally hot and humid—not to mention we were forbidden from drinking water during practice. And even once it ended it wasn't over. Immediately after the last whistle, we had to run sprints, full pads.

I wasn't sure if I was going to throw up or pass out first after my first real practice. My legs were just rubber, man. They were wobbly and my head was pounding. When the coach ended practice, some teammates were so spent that they dropped and lay down on the field, heaving, gulping in air. I didn't even take my cleats off, just staggered straight into the locker room, past players splayed on the floor and benches. I headed straight to the shower, turned it on, and sat down on the floor in full pads as the water ran over me. I had never felt that way before in my life, and it actually generated some self-doubt. This was August and classes wouldn't start for a couple weeks. Could I do this twice a day, at least five days a week?

Looking back, I realized that the coaches wanted to weed out the less determined players. There was a price to pay to stay on Coach Bryant's team. This was a bonding experience, and everybody that lasted had to earn their way.

CHAPTER SEVEN

Crowds really do feel bigger when you haven't played pro ball for a while and then take a moment to look, really look at all those people. On screen, that Orange Bowl seems packed in tight and helps my memory locate that little buzz of energy such a large crowd can give a player. I have to admit I'm getting a kick out of watching this game the same way that those pulling for the good guys must have. I feel very fortunate, in fact, that I can share both perspectives.

As I mentioned earlier, though, I'd been in big games before, while playing with Alabama. We played Oklahoma and the great Bud Wilkinson on New Year's Day for the 1963 Orange Bowl with President Kennedy up there in the stands watching. Coach Bryant had told the team in the locker room that the president was sitting on the Oklahoma side. Lee Roy Jordan, our defensive captain, and the Oklahoma captain went up into the stands to meet President Kennedy, who did the coin toss. That year was full of what, at that time, felt like historic matchups. We were ranked number one in the country when we went over to Georgia Tech and lost 7–6—a week during which Coach Bryant had worked on a two-quarterback system, concerned that Georgia Tech outmanned us with size and speed. Then, early in the game, I got a blindside hit while setting up the pass. Lights out. I came to on the bench, the left side of my body tingling. I had no idea how I got off the field. We lost that game, but the next one we beat archrival Auburn 38–0 and then went to play Oklahoma in that Orange Bowl game—in the same stadium we would play this Super Bowl—and beat them 17–0. Roll Tide!

It's strange though, watching this film now, how I couldn't remember who won the coin toss in '69 at the Super Bowl or if we even wanted the ball first. Well, the game is about to begin so I guess I'll find out. I have my pen and notepad out, and I'm feeling an odd mixture of excitement and nostalgia sitting here at the kitchen table. And not just because one of our four dogs just chased my grandson out of the room as he went running by with a bag of dog treats. I have to admit, the dogs are a little crazy. One was kidnapped and returned three years later. Two were rescues, and they're both losing their minds right now, whining and barking as the storm kicks up outside. I'm older, I've had my bell rung a few times, but I think anybody would have a hard time concentrating with this pack when they're acting up.

And then, kickoff! The Colts' Lou Michaels got some power behind it, but Earl Christy could run, boy, and his return put us in a good position.

For the first play, Weeb wanted to give Baltimore something to think about. So we shifted formations at the line of scrimmage, a little move we hadn't done all year long. That was a solid hustle, one of the most important plays in the game that no one talked about.

We had a plan that was, in a certain sense, much more AFL than NFL. We weren't rigid and inflexible. Even in life, never be too unbending. When I was growing up, Beaver Falls had two pool halls and I was a regular who stayed for hours. I knew who not to play, having watched some older sharks hustle. Pool was about making shots and getting in position to make more shots, handling pressure, but really, at that joint, I learned how valuable it was to use *all* the tricks available to win.

So Weeb had devised a play to mess with the Colts' heads, just a little bit. Nothing gimmicky, just a quick flick of unpredictability. I was comfortable with this type of game, too. As I mentioned, the magician himself, Coach Bruno, was my high school coach and he, too, was big on teaching us how to employ a deceptive offense. He really brought a street-level hustler meets magician style to my game—using physical talent and some sleight of hand to get the job done. Don't just play the team with the eyes and feet and hands—get into their heads so they aren't even sure where the ball is.

Second down and 6. Man, Snell came up behind me full stride already, charging in such a tight formation that all I had to do was reverse pivot and he was ready to tuck the rock into his arms. John Schmitt cleared the way as he cut through an opening, where Rick Volk took Snell down on our own 34. But he was so low that Snell's right knee jackhammered Volk's helmet.

It was an effective play. Snell carried for nine yards and we got our first down. Watching the broadcast, you see the cameramen focus on Snell getting up and walking toward the huddle, but glancing over his shoulder at Volk, who was on the ground. I knew Volk had been hurt when we were playing, but I didn't know the injury was that bad and the hit so violent. I certainly don't recall seeing Volk going instantly limp after making contact. He was a foundational element of the Colts' defense and such a wonderful player. Then, boom. He's out cold. To me, that was a big influence on their defensive performance.

Regardless of who was playing, though, our plan was simple: take what they give us. We were running away from the strength of their defense. That meant running the ball to both sides, deciding at the line which direction to go. Or to air it out. The Colts weren't going to change their defense for us. Why would they fix what's not broken? It's first-and-10 and we lost three yards with a Boozer run to the right. Next, I throw a swing pass to Matt Snell and he gains nine yards. But then I missed high on a subsequent pass. George Sauer was open, and I just rushed the throw. Even on my computer five decades later, it still irritates me. No wonder I hadn't watched this game in so long—I get too angry, still caught up in the mistakes.

While watching us punt, I start to recognize a certain flavor of disappointment in my gut. As a quarterback, there are few things more frustrating than missing an open receiver, and now I'm starting to feel wound up. There were no surprises from the Colts on that first series. Nothing that we didn't expect, we just didn't get it done and stopped ourselves.

* * *

On the sideline, you usually talk to the offensive coordinator first. If Coach Ewbank wanted to speak, however, he'd either send somebody for you or come over himself, to the middle where the telephones were; that's usually where I would sit, or where the defense, the linebackers, sat to talk to the coaches who were upstairs in the press box.

After that first series, I headed to the phone and confirmed that the Colts didn't give us anything out of the ordinary. We hung up and I was itching to get back out there. One thing you rarely get to see from the television broadcasts, even today, are the players' faces. But when under center and looking up over those linemen, you'd be surprised by how much you can make out behind those masks. Part of the art of quarterbacking is not only reading defenses, but also reading emotions. Eyes are one of the biggest giveaways. They show if a player is shaken up or in pain. A certain expression can sometimes tell you everything. Looking back, I could have picked up on Rick Volk's injury and tried to test him sooner, put him in a one-on-one situation with a speedy receiver.

We were prepared and not expecting the Colts to do anything but play their best. That feeling—that confidence—came from studying the heck out of film and the seemingly never-ending pile of notes our coaches gave us. But studying for games was of course nothing new and had been a process I'd taken pride in since being in the audio-visual club in high school. I like to be prepared.

For the Tennessee game my sophomore year, I was playing with a charley horse in my thigh from the week earlier and had been unable to practice on defense. One of the advantages of getting those defensive reps in in the week leading up to the game is that you have a chance to see and react to looks your opponent will be using against you. We had to know both an offensive and defensive position back then, and while I rarely played anything other than QB during a game, I ended up at right cornerback for one series. Known for their single wing, Tennessee ran the ball in my direction, and I swear it looked like the whole team was headed my way. During practice our coaches had been working with us on what keys to read and which player we were responsible for...but I hadn't been in on those practices. As the cavalry was coming at me, I took a couple of steps up and missed my assignment. Meanwhile, one of their receivers slipped right by me and got wide open. By the time I turned, I was in a chase position, he was in the lead, and a pass was floating right over my head. Fortunately, Billy Piper, our free safety, was able to get over there in time and save the day by knocking the pass down. I was close—I've argued for years that I caught up and got a finger on the ball—but right away defensive assistant Gene Stallings took me out of the game and I headed straight for the bench.

Coach Stallings, who would later become head coach at Alabama and win a National Championship, had a unique way of communicating with us. He was a good-sized man and he'd throw his arm around you, so you couldn't help but pay attention.

He started: "Gosh, darn it, Namath, what were you doing out there?"

I said, "Coach, I'm sorry, I didn't practice all week. I didn't get to see that play."

I was stuttering and stammering, and even though it was a legitimate excuse, nobody wants to hear anything but an assurance that the same mistake won't happen again. He didn't waste any more time on the subject, though. Just gave me a stern look and walked back to the sidelines. I wasn't expecting to ever play defense that week, but I knew I had been fooled on that play due to a lack of preparation. It was an awful feeling.

I was big on preparation, as I've mentioned already, and there were only a few times I didn't feel ready. Once was when I was told that my dad was dying in the hospital and I went back and forth to Pittsburgh three times in the course of a week. We were getting ready to play the Colts in Baltimore in 1972, but my mind wasn't on the game and I had done almost nothing to get ready. So, I'm sitting in front of my locker, looking at my playbook. It's an hour or two before kickoff and I'm trying to get caught up on the whole game plan. I wasn't prepared and I was miserable, not knowing the short yardage and basically the entire offensive game plan.

But that game...together, the Colts and our Jets combined for more passing yardage than any other two teams in the history of pro football up to that point. Our guys and I connected for six touchdowns through the air as we went on to beat the Colts 44–34. We only completed fifteen passes out of twenty-eight, but they accounted for 490 yards. We would think that the fans, regardless of what team they were pulling for, would've loved that contest. Even more memorable is the fact that the last two passes were TDs of seventy-nine and eighty yards. I knew the Colts were expecting us to milk the clock and run the ball. When we got in the huddle, I told the guys, "Look, they think we're gonna try to run the clock out. All right? Well, we're gonna go Pro Right, Sixty Go." That verbiage means that the wide receivers both on the right and left sides would try to run past the defending back, and our tight end would run down the middle of the field past his defender.

Instinctively, I just knew they were going to blitz, so I called maximum protection and sent three receivers out. I hit Rich Caster down the middle as he outran his strong safety coverage for a seventy-nine-yard touchdown. We kicked off and Unitas and his Colts methodically drove down the field and scored again. We went out on the field and I said, "Well, they think we're still going to run the clock down." We flipped the formation and I managed to hit Caster as he outran the safety again for eighty yards. By the way, Richard Caster was the fastest tight end in the league that year. His nickname was Hooks. He had come as a wide-out rookie before the Jets converted him into a tight end.

On that second one, Mike Curtis, the middle linebacker—they called him Mad Dog and he was one of the best linebackers you could play against—was in a chase position. When Caster caught the ball, he started running with Curtis in chase. Eventually, Curtis made a dive to try and catch Caster, but fell short, and while facedown on the turf, he started pounding both fists on the ground. That was a satisfying sight to see. I ran over to Hooks, hands down, palms up, and he gave me one of my favorite down-low slaps.

But I wasn't prepared for that game. When it was over the media asked questions: "How'd you guys do this?" I'm sitting wondering about my dad now, and I look at the reporter and think, By the grace of God, I have no other idea...

Back in my kitchen, watching myself on the sideline, while our defense takes the field, I can see that I was focused, and I remember feeling ready mentally. Almost immediately, though, Baltimore starts advancing the ball and they look as dominant as they had all season. I mean, man! They're making some good gains. They're looking good.

Then there's a break and the old-style white font that NBC once used shows up on the screen, listing the day's roster. I see one position, SE, that gives me pause before remembering some older terms: split end. You don't hear that term too much these days. The split end was on the weak side of the formation and the flanker was always on the strong side of the formation. The strong side being dictated by the formation where the tight end lines up. But the graphics flash off suddenly, and the Colts keep marching.

Then I see Johnny Sample, who is already walking around trash talking. Man, he was good. Johnny liked to talk, a lot more than anyone else. Gerry Philbin and Jim Hudson might say some things, too, but Johnny—he would put in that special effort to help get into the other teams' heads. The Colts had their verbal snipers as well, but unexpectedly, even after all the headlines and hoopla about my "guarantee," I didn't hear a single peep about it on the field. I don't know, but it seems as if it didn't register much with the Colts. If the score had been different with them ahead, then I'm sure I would have heard something about my guarantee. I might have even heard something from my own teammates.

* * *

Coming out of college, there was a chance those teammates could have been NFL players instead of the AFL's Jets. Back then, nobody prepared or walked you through the process of the draft. I had no idea what to expect;

neither did anyone else. For such a major life moment where so much can ride on making the right decision, it's weird how unaware I was.

I knew nothing about my draft. They didn't do it on television or the radio. You found out when they called on the phone. There was no internet or texting in December, 1964, obviously, and no agents floating around colleges or even the pros back then.

Considering how many players were drafted from his teams, I'm sure Coach Bryant had a much better sense of how it all worked than I did. I can't even remember who called first to let me know what position I was in the draft. It wasn't even clear who called me to let me know that I was picked by the AFL Jets and the NFL Cardinals.

People like to ask if I was there at the draft, but there was no "there." No gathering, no glitz, no showbiz. I wasn't waiting by any phone, partly because I didn't know what day it was held. Maybe it was printed somewhere in the papers, but I never saw anything. I knew I wanted to play pro ball and that I was hoping to get a chance, and I didn't care with who. It just wasn't something I really felt like I had a lot of control over.

I only thought about getting some help after two representatives of the St. Louis Cardinals showed up in suits, unannounced. I was still going to school in Alabama and came back to my dorm room. I was sitting on my bed and another player came up and said I had some guys down in the lobby who wanted to see me.

I wasn't expecting anybody, and I hadn't been contacted. I walked down and had no idea who they were, but they introduced themselves as representatives from the NFL

Cardinals. The NFL held their draft earlier than the AFL so I didn't know what or even if an AFL team would pick me. There was a war going on between the leagues, who were each battling for the best college players and willing to do whatever necessary to get them signed before their rival league did.

I was still just twenty-one years old with no business experience. These serious-looking men introduced themselves and we all kind of stood around awkwardly in the lobby of my dorm. I didn't really have a quiet place to invite them, so the only spot to talk was in my room. I invited them upstairs. I shared a room with Butch Henry, our tight end. It was small, with two beds, a dresser, AC, no hanging closet, and a bathroom down the hall.

They came in and I invited them to sit on my bed. I had respect for Butch so I didn't offer them his bed. But once they sat, I went across the room and sat on his bunk.

These two representatives from the St. Louis Cardinals—one was the president of the team and the other the general manager—told me that they had drafted me and asked me what kind of contract I was looking for.

But Coach Bryant was always looking after his players, and he had brought it up to me in the locker room after our last regular season game against Auburn. Coach Bryant came over to where I was helping Steve Sloan put a sock on because he had hurt his knee—that was how I got to play a little bit in that game with my own injured knee. Coach Bryant was a big man, six-foot-four or so, and he looked down at me. He asked if I had any idea what kind of contract I was thinking about.

"You know these pro guys are going to be approaching

you to play for them. Do you know what you are going to ask for?"

"Well, Coach, I hear Don Trull signed with the Houston Oilers for a hundred grand last year. I was thinking that."

Coach took a big ol' draw off his Pall Mall and looked up at the ceiling, thinking for a moment. "Well, you go ahead and ask them for two hundred thousand. Better place to start."

Right there, one of the most important people in my life and development just doubled my contract. He cared about his players. No, not just his players, he seemed to care about everybody that stuck with him for at least four years. That was my sole piece of negotiating advice up to that point.

Now I was sitting there, marveling. Damn, two hundred grand? That's crazy! I couldn't get it out of my mouth. Seriously. The suit guys were sitting on my bed, I guess thinking the negotiations had begun, but I was just trying to build some courage to spit out that ridiculous amount. I mean, men at the mill in Beaver Falls were making maybe six, seven grand a year. Finally, I said, in a slightly sheepish voice, "Two hundred thousand dollars."

Then their acting began. Boy, were these guys hamming it up.

"Oh, my God!" Suit Number One said and looked incredulously at Suit Number Two. "Two hundred thousand dollars?"

Suit Number Two: "Can you believe this kid?"

But I wasn't finished yet. Their bad performance bolstered me a bit, but I was still nervous that I had asked for too much.

Suit Number One: "Who does he think he is to…" He looked at me. "Two. Hundred. Thousand."

"Yes, sir," I said. "And a new car."

Then both Suits slapped their heads. They were going all in.

Suit Number Two: "Oh! He wants a car!"

Suit Number One: "Well, what kind of car?"

Larry Patterson, my friend and old teammate from Beaver Falls, was playing for West Texas State University. He had called and as we got talking about the draft, he asked, "What kinda short you gonna get?"

A short is what we called a boss car. I didn't have one picked out—yet.

"A Lincoln Continental, man," he said. "A Lincoln Continental convertible, man. It is bad! It's got barn doors."

I didn't even know what it looked like. Not only that, but I also had no idea what barn doors were.

"I'd like a Lincoln Continental," I said.

"Yeah, suuuuure," Suit One said. "A Lin-coln Con-tin-en-tal!"

They made me feel embarrassed. Had I pushed it too far? We were just throwing around ridiculous amounts. I had no real-life experiences to understand what that amount of money really meant.

Then Suit Number Two said, "Okay."

The acting just stopped right there as Suit Number One opened his briefcase and started taking out paperwork.

"Wait a minute," I say. "I can't sign anything."

They did not want to leave that little room without my signature. Coach Bryant, again, God bless him, had told me not to take anything from either professional team that had drafted me. Nothing! Not even a Coca-Cola. We still had the Orange Bowl and if I took anything as payment I'd have become ineligible to play. I would be breaking the rules and

I knew from personal experience what a stickler for rules Coach Bryant was.

But not everybody held themselves to that Coach Bryant standard. This was a bidding war and they did sign guys who still played in college. But I was aware that some AFL team was probably going to draft me so I wasn't about to sign anything, anyway. The AFL and NFL would even take prospects and hide them so other agents wouldn't be able to find them until after contracts were signed.

After the meeting with the Cardinals, I knew I needed representation. I called my friend Mike Bite, a fellow A-Club member and a legal eagle from Birmingham, Alabama. When the Jets drafted me, Mike contacted Mr. Werblin and they made plans to meet in California. The Jets were playing San Diego and I had a hole in my schedule. See, after the last game prior to a bowl game, teams had a couple weeks off and NCAA rules prohibited continual practicing. The last game was in November and you couldn't start practicing for the bowl game until the third week of December.

So the Jets contacted Mike and he bought the tickets, not them. We flew out to LA and were met at the airport by a chauffeur in a big ole limousine, the likes of which we'd only seen in movies. He drove us to the Beverly Hills Hotel where we met Mr. Werblin, who just flat-out starts the first meeting with, "Well, I'm not interested in what the other league is offering, just know that we're going to beat them. We'll give you more than the other side will."

He opened a hundred grand above what Suit Number One and Suit Number Two had heart attacks over. He came in at $300,000. Mike and I looked at each other and asked Mr. Werblin if we could go into another room to talk this over. We both thought the three hundred grand was a great offer and we should go for it, but I wanted to do something for my family back home in Beaver Falls. And I still wanted that new Lincoln Continental convertible. Mr. Werblin agreed and barely seemed fazed as he agreed to everything that Mike and I asked for, and that's how the whole package came to $427,000 for three years.

Coach Weeb Ewbank was also the general manager of the Jets and he knew his personnel on the team. They structured my contract so my salary was $25,000, comparable and even less than some of my new teammates' pay, so the veterans on the team couldn't negotiate against it, since a few of them were still making more than the rookie, salary-wise. That extra money was all a bonus, so I was thusly born a Bonus Baby. And my Lincoln showed up forest-green with a white top. My brothers Bob and Frank, and my sister's husband, all landed scouting jobs.

After my verbal commitment to Mr. Werblin, Mike had to go back to the Cardinals and tell them that I was going to sign with the Jets. The Cardinal representatives asked Mr. Bite if I was strongly interested in New York City, because if so they could negotiate a deal with the NFL's New York Giants. But I was convinced at that point that Mr. Werblin and Coach Ewbank were the people I wanted to work with. I was going to be a Jet.

CHAPTER EIGHT

Time to get up and stretch the legs, now featuring two artificial knees, a new hip, and an abnormal-looking left hamstring. That last injury was due to a 1973 water-skiing accident in the Bay of Five Pirates at Great Harbour Cay in the Bahamas. I severed two of my three hamstring muscles in my left leg. Just as I was getting pulled up on the water, the rope snapped, twisting my body to the right while my left leg fell behind and took all the pressure. The pain was sudden and near consuming, and when they hoisted me out of the water and into the boat, I was already in shock, shaking uncontrollably.

A buddy of mine had a private plane on the island. He heard about my injury and wanted to fly me out, but the landing strip didn't have lights so the plane couldn't leave after dark. He flew me to New York the next morning. Blood had been filling my leg up all night, and by then the back of it had turned purplish black. The two severed muscles had rolled down into a ball the size of a grapefruit.

I met the Jets' Dr. Nicholas at Lenox Hill hospital and

he examined my leg. I was mentally prepared for another operation.

"We're not going to operate."

I asked why, and he said that he had studied this injury, and the method required a body cast up to the chest to limit movement. "It'll heal, and the only reason you need a hamstring muscle is to run." He smiled. "And you're a quarterback, Joe, you don't need to run."

Dr. Nicholas had been there since my first knee surgery, taking out a cyst, shaving the meniscus, and repairing three ligaments. Much later on, after numerous knee surgeries, he would mention that I had the knees of a seventy-year-old man. I'm seventy-five right now and, boy, my knees hurt a heck of a lot less than at Super Bowl III. I've had twenty-six years of generally pain-free knees.

But I can still remember how Dr. Nicholas walked into the recovery room as my head was clearing after my first knee surgery in 1965. All three of my brothers were there, but I was barely awake.

"Surgery went really well, Joe. You're going to see a lot of improvement with your knee and the pain should decrease considerably."

He talked me and my brothers through the procedure and explained that I would naturally lose a lot of leg strength and how important rehabilitation was going to be in getting back on the field.

I nodded, still groggy. Recovery. Whatever—I could barely keep my eyes open and my leg throbbed in pain.

"And—we are going to start now."

He took my leg and lifted it up by the heel, the heavy ankle-to-groin plaster cast making it awkward, but the movement didn't hurt. Until he said, "Good. I'm going to take my hand away and you need to hold your leg up. We've got to work that quadricep muscle and prevent any more atrophy."

Well, I was WIDE awake when he let go. I thought my leg was going to burst.

I was holding my breath using every muscle in my body to keep it elevated. And there was no way I was gonna drop that leg with Sonny, Bob, and Frank there. The only way I held that damn leg up was because my brothers were watching. I wouldn't have had the determination to hold it up without them. Or maybe my ego just wouldn't have cared with anyone else.

I had my eyes closed, all my concentration focused on keeping that leg up.

"Okay, you can let it down now," he said. "Slowly, take it easy."

I was moved into a hospital room for the next two weeks and change. Well, not exactly a standard-issue hospital room. To the left of my bed was a portable cooler bar filled with Rheingold beer, a sponsor of the Jets. On top of the cooler was a bottle of Bell's 12 Scotch, the brand that Mr. Werblin drank, and also a bottle of Courvoisier brandy for Dr. Nicholas. There was also a nice bottle of Kentucky bourbon for whoever. If I looked to my right, I was met with a beautiful view of Park Avenue.

My leg was put in traction and they began pumping in the morphine. That was just a common procedure back then, although they warned it was going to be difficult to wean me off the drug. I tried to resist asking for the stuff, but that made me aware of my physical craving for it. I'd never

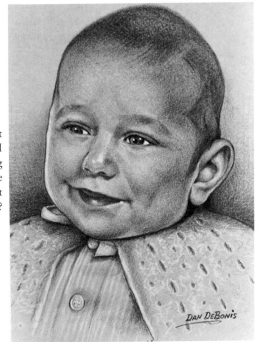

I've been told this is me at just three months old, but I have a tough time believing that. Looks more like twelve to fifteen months to me, but what do I know?

DAN DeBONIS

Sister Rita is in front, styling with her rolled cuffs, saddle shoes, and scarf. I'm on the left in the striped shirt, then cousin Barbara Lee and brother Bob being spiffy. We're going somewhere or visiting someone.

This was taken on a brisk fall day while visiting relatives in Massillon, Ohio. From left to right: Franklin, Bob holding me captive, cousins Paul Samuel and Barbara Lee, and Rita.

You think Mom got her hair done here? Naw, she always looked like this while answering my fan mail. She loved interacting with fans and even wrote her own book!

I was a junior wearing number 15 on my 1959 high school underclassmen football team. This was Coach Larry Bruno's (whistle around neck) first season with the Fighting Tigers. Our athletic director, Bill Ross, is behind him in the white shirt.

Crossing home plate at the 1961 Western Pennsylvania Interscholastic Athletic League semifinals game. There was no fence in the outfield, and I hit a long shot over the left fielder's head and hustled around the bags for a stand-up homerun. We won the game and went on to win the championship at Forbes Field in Pittsburgh, home of the Pirates.

Left to right: Sonny, Bobby, Frank, and me, Christmas 1962, right before they drove me to the Pittsburgh airport for the Orange Bowl. I went from snowflakes the size of silver dollars falling from the sky to palm trees and blooming flowers. Oh, by the way: Alabama 17, Oklahoma 0.

I started caddying during the summers when I was twelve and started playing golf in college. If it's not the most difficult game I have ever played, I don't know what is.

In the locker room with my favorite drummer and one of the loves of my life, who I nicknamed Jumpin' Jack Flash—Jack Scarangella—and whose mentor was the great Buddy Rich.

On the field for a home game in Bryant-Denny Stadium in Tuscaloosa. My eyes go right to my granddaughter Jemma. We had a great time with the Tide fans. My oldest friend and my first agent, Mike Bite, who helped me negotiate my rookie Jets contract, is sporting the 'Bama hat. Mike has an even more important job here—we entrusted him with Jemma's rabbit, Buns. Roll Tide! (© Jessica Namath)

Another day for Jessica and me at Gulfstream Park racetrack in North Miami with one of my dearest friends, Joe Hirsch. He was not only my first roommate in New York, but he was also instrumental in helping me learn the nuts and bolts of the Big Apple, and life itself. He was known as a class act at every track throughout the world.

Joking around with my daughter Olivia Rose at her favorite place on earth, Disney World. Heck, we all love it there!

Some of our New York Jets Texas studs. From left to right: wide receiver George Sauer, tight end Big Boy Pete Lammons, me, wide receiver and Hall of Famer Don Maynard, and wide receiver Bake Turner, who also doubled as team vocalist and guitarist. My first season at training camp he sang our team's new fight song: "There's No Business Like Show Business."

Taken at the Joe Namath–John Dockery Football Camp, which ran for forty-six years. John was a defensive back on our championship team and approached me about starting a camp where we could pass on the lessons we learned in football and teach boys and girls about the most important game of all: life. I'm still grateful to the campers and parents who inspired me and helped me improve my game.
Back row, left to right: Winston Hill, Victor Hobson, Eric Coleman, Dave Herman. I'm in the front with daughter Jessica and John.
(© Shari Fitzgerald)

There's nothin' like gameday in Tuscaloosa! Jessica, granddaughter Jemma Rose, and I were guests of athletic director Bill Battle, who also happened to be our tight end on the 1961 Alabama National Championship team.

Who would have thought that we'd last this long? Good buddy Jimmy Walsh and I have been together since 1961. He's been looking out for me like some Irish-Hungarian guardian angel with a touch of Yosemite Sam's temper. If it wasn't for Jimmy, who knows where I'd be. (© Tommy Garcia)

I'm starting the fourth quarter of the big game and so thankful to have my family team with me. Left to right: John John, Jessica, Jemma, the birthday boy, Olivia, and Natalia. (© Charles Modica)

Soaking in the positive vibes of my spiritual connection to the natural wonders and creatures on this earth and in this universe. (© Jessica Namath)

experienced my body demanding something so hard, fighting me for it—physically it seemed to be relentless. But my inner voice wanted to beat it, and gradually the craving subsided. I didn't know what addiction meant back then, and that was the first time I recognized my body having a reaction to a substance. It scared the hell out of me. I prayed for strength, and what connection I had to my higher power grew and remains strong to this day.

I left the hospital around two weeks later, twenty-seven pounds lighter. I do recall a nice nurse wheeling me out onto the curb where I caught a taxi to the airport for my flight to Birmingham. My knee was never back to where it had been before the injury, but it was much more stable.

I trusted Dr. Nicholas, and Coach Bruno had already showed me the importance of having a doctor who understands how you push yourself and what's necessary to heal properly. In my senior year in a high school game against a tough Ambridge football team, this guy got a really good lick in—he hit me, wrapped me up in his arms, and we both fell with my left shoulder the first thing to hit the ground.

That hurt.

Lying there I felt the pain radiate from my shoulder. I was helped up, keeping my left arm close to my body, across my chest. Since it was now fourth down I came off the field. Coach Bruno saw me in pain and asked what was wrong. I told him, but said I was fine to play and for the next series of downs, I went back in.

We won the game, but afterward, when I was on the bus, my buddy Whitey Harris came up and, unaware of my injury, gave me a celebratory slap on my shoulder. I have no shame in saying that my scream was...alarming.

Coach Bruno and my dad took me to the Beaver Falls Providence hospital. I sat in the emergency room as the doctor on duty examined me. He felt the lump on my shoulder and I winced and sucked in a sharp breath.

"You did this playing football?" he asked as he felt the injured area. "Well, you're finished playing this season."

I actually couldn't process what he was saying. No more football this season? It can't be over.

Coach Bruno immediately said, "Nope. No."

We walked to the parking lot, and Coach Bruno turned to my father and me.

"Tomorrow we see Doc Berkman. He's a renowned orthopedist." He saw how concerned I was and nodded at me. "Let's see what he says before we jump to any conclusions about the rest of the season."

Doc Berkman's office was about six miles away, and Coach Bruno drove me over the next day. I sat in his office as he gently felt my shoulder, asked me to raise my arm, rotate it as far as I could.

"How's it look?" Coach asked.

"Ligament tear. First-degree separation. He can play again."

That was when I learned my first lesson in injuries— what a doctor says is not set in stone. Even back then there were innovative and progressive doctors who didn't look at an injury as some sort of end, but instead as an unfortunate hurdle that needed attention and adaptation to overcome. There's a psychology with injuries and it really makes a difference if a doctor understands that.

Doc Berkman cut two pads out of rubber, each about a half-inch thick, with a hole in the middle like a big donut.

He put it over my shoulder and explained how to tape it when I played. By Wednesday, five days after separating my shoulder, I was pretty much full speed in practice and the pain had subsided. I didn't miss a game the rest of the year and we finished 9-0. And every time I feel the lump on my shoulder, I remember that season.

* * *

I let the Super Bowl footage start playing back where we left off, as I hear my daughters and grandkids playing in the other room. They are the loves of my life, of course. My attention snaps back to the game, though, as I see the Colts moving the ball against our defense. That is until a pass that would have gone for a decent gain is quite simply dropped. We got some breaks. There's good luck in life and there's some bad luck, but hopefully, you'll take advantage of the good luck. And with that, it's fourth down on the Colts' first drive. Now Lou Michaels is going on to kick a field goal. Lou, who almost broke up Frankie's a few days earlier with his own guarantee, lines up for the field goal attempt and misses. On the sidelines, I watched, pretty sure he would make it but pulling for him to miss. Lou certainly had the leg to make it from that distance. But being a passer, I know the flight of the ball is influenced by the wind from time to time. And the wind was certainly gusting that day.

The Jets were used to playing with occasional foul weather at Shea. I hated all winds, unless I was flying a kite or they were coming at my back. Thankfully, pregame warm-ups allow you to gauge how the conditions outside will influence your throws. But sometimes the gusts get so bad, there isn't much you can do except release the ball and hope. Once, in a 1974 game in War Memorial Stadium against the Buffalo Bills, their quarterback, Joe Ferguson, and I struggled in a downpour, heavy rain for the whole game with a forty-mile-per-hour *crosswind*. Neither one of us completed a forward pass until the fourth quarter. I'm complaining about the weather only because we lost.

In Super Bowl III, there was wind, but it wasn't a *major* factor in the passing or kicking game. By our second series there was a game flow rhythm. On the sidelines, every time the offense came off the field, I would either talk to Coach Ewbank or a teammate, and then definitely get on the headset with our offensive coordinator. The press box is situated high enough to provide a view of the whole field. Both the defensive and offensive play callers need input from somebody with a whole-field view. Standing on the sidelines is the worst seat in the house—you can't see all the action. I'd sit down to conserve energy, though. I took the weight off my legs whenever possible, and hardly ever saw Maynard, Snell, Sauer, Boozer, or Mathis standing up when they could sit on the bench.

Regardless of position, these guys all became receivers in the passing game. It's hard to play against an offense that's spreading the ball around. And the sheer variety of receivers getting in on the action impresses me to this today. Matt Snell caught one early and then Pete Lammons. I went to Sauer on the next pass and overthrew him—no, that was Mathis, our running back! See, we moved the ball around—we threw to who's open. The Colts were very good on defense at taking away the offensive team's most dangerous weapon. But we had a group of receivers who could exploit that.

Early on, we took a deep shot. Maynard got a step on the defender and almost snagged a slight overthrow on a go route. (By the way, my English teacher in college stated that there's only one way to pronounce that word, and it's "root." But I never heard anybody in football say it that way.) Regardless, that route let the Colts know that Maynard could go deep. I realize, looking at it on the screen now, that big Bubba Smith definitely influenced that throw with his proximity to killing me and all. But even with that, Maynard could chase balls down. During this game, he knew he wasn't 100 percent. We knew. But the Colts didn't. The injury was never announced, so they needed to rotate to his side, pay him special attention with two guys, short and deep. Every team had to give special respect to Maynard and his sneaky speed. The Colts' secondary had been rotating to Don's side, but on that particular incomplete pass, they didn't make the adjustment. But after that, every single time, they double covered him, short and long.

Then the Colts started coming with their safety blitzes. On one of the early ones, I recognized they had more rushers than we had blockers, so I made a "hot read" and flicked the ball to Sauer. These reads took coordination. If George wasn't seeing the safety blitz, then I had nowhere to go with the ball, except to eat it or throw it away. Toss it into the dirt downfield or out of bounds.

Third-and-9 now. George was open and the protection was great. He was right there, about fifteen yards downfield, and I saw him clearly on his square-in route, drifting perfectly into the empty pocket on the left side of the zone defense. My sense of urgency was too quick, and the throw sailed over his head. I didn't need to get rid of the ball so fast. That urgency was wrong. I remember being frustrated with myself in the game, and now I am again. I rewind the play just to confirm what a buffoon I was. But that emotional pain is no surprise to me. It's been almost half a century and there are times when I'm in the swimming pool doing my laps—one of the most mind-numbing activities I can imagine—and to pass the time and keep my brain sharp, I list the states and capitals alphabetically frontward and then backward, and out of nowhere that damn pass will come bustin' through and break my focus. That's just one of the negative plays that do this to me. Five hours afterward, five days, five decades—memories of the misses and losses never seem to fade.

So that leads to fourth down. Another failed drive and time to punt. I'm watching Curley's punt trying to remember anything I felt while on the sidelines, when out of nowhere comes Matt Snell—he's covering on punts! I never realized that. Where do you see a starting running back covering on special teams these days? Not to mention one who will end up rushing for over a hundred yards in the game?

I jot down a couple notes as the Colts take the field and right away drop a catchable ball. John Mackey even, which is surprising in hindsight. Sure, everyone drops a pass once in a while, but he was one of the best tight ends that ever played. He's a Hall of Famer.

The first quarter is winding down and I'm starting to get agitated with myself for not having played better. Meanwhile, the defense was dominating, with Johnny Sample taking the lead. Before long, the Colts were punting again—but this time it was a great kick that rolls dead inside our 4, and I sure as heck don't remember being backed up that close to our own goal line.

After two gutsy runs by Snell, we got the ball out to what

looks like our 13-yard line. We only needed one yard to get the first, but I ended up going with a pass and hit Sauer for three yards. But he was nailed quickly by defensive back Lenny Lyles and dropped the ball. Today, that would be ruled an incomplete pass. The refs said it was a fumble though, and the Colts recovered. I rewind it, and I still can't tell if George had complete possession. But if George didn't think he caught it, I imagine he'd have argued it. And he doesn't seem to be putting up much of a fight.

The Colts got the ball just twelve yards from our end zone. I have no recollection what I was doing while Philbin tackled Jerry Hill for a one-yard loss on the first play of that drive, which also happened to be the last play of the first quarter.

I take a moment to reassess how we played in the first quarter and feel disappointed in my performance. Not that I was playing poorly, but I remember performing a bit better than what that tape is showing. There are, however, two words on our championship ring for a reason, and they were lessons that Coach Ewbank never stopped preaching: execution— which means working together, getting it done—and poise.

Watch that game and you won't see any Jet losing their temper. Johnny Sample, meanwhile, was doing his best to get under the thin skin of any Colt player. He was a world-class athlete, champion at taunting, and a poise breaker. On our end, though, nobody was costing the team a penalty because of something stupid like a late hit or unsportsmanlike conduct.

When they play dirty, we keep our poise.

An interception? We keep our poise.

A fumble? We keep our poise, all the way.

And we're always executing.

But if for some reason, we don't? We keep our poise.

CHAPTER NINE

We changed end zones for the next quarter, play starts and Colts halfback Tom Matte barreled five more yards toward the goal line. Now, if you don't already know what happens next, you'd think the result of this drive was imminent: the Colts, on our 6-yard line, were going to score a touchdown. But if you were to think such a thing, then you don't know the 1968 New York Jets defense. They were fighters.

Earl Morrall did a quick drop, looked to his left, and fired. But number 62, our middle linebacker, Al Atkinson, read the quarterback's eyes, threw his body near horizontal, and extended his right arm, stretching his hand to get a fingertip on the ball, misdirecting the pass to the back shoulder of the receiver. I should mention here that this was news to me, having no idea on game day that Al had in fact tipped the ball. Because of his efforts, though, the pigskin bounced off Colts tight end Tom Mitchell and high up into the air, where tens of millions waited to see where it landed, which just so happened to be the hands of our Randy Beverly, who made a diving catch.

Ball is ours. And I'm not going to say we got lucky, because Atkinson and Beverly both made terrific plays. But I sure wouldn't want to be stuck in that position again.

We got possession back on our 20-yard line and I remember this: I called Flank Right Nineteen. The Colts were shifted to our tight end side so I had Snell go the other way. On the next play again, we got the same look from the Colts so we did the same thing. Flank Right Nineteen. We essentially ran the same play a third time, but as a draw. Running similar plays repeatedly wasn't part of the plan going into the game, but if they're not stopping you, then wear it out. And our left tackle, Winston Hill, and Bob Talamini, our left guard, were doing such a terrific job of getting off the ball and blocking that not going behind them would have been a big mistake. I might add that Boozer and Mathis never missed their block on the play Nineteen-straight either.

Again, the Colts weren't going to change for us. They planned on kicking our butts. Maybe that was part of the overconfidence, maybe it was just the way their coach insisted on playing, but they didn't come into this game thinking it was going to be different than any other game in their season. This is how they were used to playing and what success we're having with Nineteen-straight is not surprising. Offensively, we were designed to be flexible. Sometimes that got us into trouble and other times, especially when playing a team very set in their ways, it could be an advantage.

* * *

The networks sure don't have nearly the commercial breaks during the game like they do now. I get it—that's a big revenue source for the league. It was and remains one for me, too. I had some good luck with ads that helped establish me and put my face out there without a helmet and face mask. One of my first ones that got a lot of attention showed me shaving off my Fu Manchu mustache.

The AFL could sometimes be uptight, and in 1968, the older generation considered you a counterculture freak or hippie if you had long hair or a beard. Well, Jesus Christ himself had long hair. You know, you look in history. What? You're going to judge somebody on their hair or beard? I just think that that's—I would use the word "simple," but it's borderline stupid. Anyway, after a practice in Shea, a bunch of us were in the shower room and decided not to shave until we made the playoffs. This was after we lost early games against Buffalo and Denver, the two last-place teams in the American Football League. I had a big part in both losses, by the way, having thrown five interceptions in each. I had seventeen interceptions the whole year, and ten of them came in two games against last-place teams.

We clinched the championship, and Coach Ewbank put this letter up on the bulletin board; it was the commissioner of the American Football League demanding that Weeb make his team shave their facial hair. But the date was two months earlier. Weeb knew his team. He knew his personnel. I mean he was a believer in rules, but he accepted this was not going to fly. And it showed me that he trusted his team. He wasn't going to upset that applecart and I think he was proud of the guys finding a way to stick together. He appreciated the unity.

But now it was time to shave, so I was talking to my friend and personal advisor Jimmy, who now handled my work deals, and I said, "Let's call somebody and see if they want to do a commercial with this."

He arranged something with Schick and we shaved it off in that commercial. Only got one take. It was real.

The idea about wearing pantyhose wasn't mine, but an ad agency approached us with storyboards and I got a kick out of it. I knew it was the right thing to do after I talked with our secretary who said her daddy wouldn't like it because football players shouldn't do things like this. Was she serious? Jimmy and I looked at each other.

"Wait a minute. This is a good company with a good product and it's fun. Let's go for it."

After that we were fully committed to the commercial. However, the first time I actually saw it I instantly felt nauseous. That quickly subsided once I remembered the paycheck.

And I just kept going and having fun. I did commercials for Hamilton Beach, Braniff Airways, Brut 33, Dingo boots, Ovaltine, La-Z-Boy, and Farrah Fawcett rubbed Noxzema cream all over my face in one of the earliest Super Bowl ads. Hey, we're men playing a game here—let's have a good time.

I did turn down a seminude offer from *Cosmopolitan,* though. The star who didn't was one of the world's biggest movie actors, Burt Reynolds. I got to know him later on as the former Florida State Seminole football player living only a couple miles from my current home.

* * *

Snell kept steadily gaining yardage: one yard, then seven, then six, then another twelve. We were in such a rhythm that I didn't even notice him head to the sidelines for a breather. He'd been getting a workout. So much so they'd bring over the oxygen, this big bag billowing up and then deflating as you put on that face mask and start sucking in.

Mathis was playing both positions, fullback and halfback, and all year long he'd been coming in for Snell and Boozer.

First-and-10, it feels great even seeing that now. I dropped back for a pass play and did something that my memory has forgotten, perhaps with good reason. I run the play back and watch myself fake the handoff before dropping back and tossing the ball to my left, targeting Sauer. But Don Shinnick, who set the record for career interceptions by a linebacker, got under the pass and by some miracle dropped what could have been a game-changing pick. Man, even when you're watching a game where you win, those mistakes are still painful. And look at all the Jets kneeling on the sideline, keeping off the white—I had a good, poised audience on that play. They didn't even seem to wince.

After seeing this next play, I remember how big the completion was, even though it didn't look like much in the moment. They tried to blitz. They tried to fool our blocking by coming with an all-out rush and covering our fullback with a defensive end. Billy Mathis was in for Snell, and was supposed to be covered by Bubba Smith. Smith dropped back to cover Billy, but wasn't quite able to run him down, as I led Billy to the sideline with the ball before taking a shove hard enough to make me hit the deck from Mike Curtis. It was no big deal.

Looks like then we start rolling. It was first down and I called a pass play, the same square in-route that I had overthrown to George earlier in the game. This time I hit him right between the numbers, giving us the sort of gain that can't help but make me break out in a smile right here in my house as I'm watching. Then they show a replay and I get giddy seeing how beautiful of a route Sauer ran, getting the defensive back off-balance with a juke to the left before squaring in to the hole in the defense.

It's first-and-10 again, and I note how deep Lyles is playing Sauer, so I had him do a quick out, the play that George caught and fumbled on in the first quarter. This, I believe, was a "check with me," an on-the-line call. I threw the pass, and Lyles nearly got to the ball. Lyles kind of set me up on that play. On his alignment, he was giving me a misread. He laid off George knowing I would take advantage of his depth and I would call the quick out, which I did. Considering the Colts had rotated the defense toward Maynard's side, I didn't expect him to even get that close. But Lyles was a good cornerback and he read the route, he read the aggressive pass protection from our offensive line. I'm thankful I threw a fastball because any less heat on the pass, Lyles would have been headed to a touchdown and six points.

Then, two plays later, I see something else I never realized happened on game day. After I hit Snell on a swing pass, he rumbled about twelve yards down the field where he was tackled and for a brief moment lost the ball! I hadn't known that he'd fumbled when I was on the field. And you think I'd have seen or heard everything about the game over the years, but that's somebody else picking and choosing what mattered.

You can tell we're smelling the end zone now, only nine yards in front of us. Watching the broadcast, I don't remember exactly what play I run next, but when I see myself simply handing the ball off to Snell, I'm not at all surprised. Take what they give us, remember?

The next huddle, however, I distinctly remember the play before it comes on my screen.

Again, you've got to speak clearly and simply in huddles. Everybody bends down keeping real still. "All right, listen up. We're running Nineteen Reach. They're going to be in a tight five-one right. Nineteen Reach. Listen up, we're going on the first sound. You hear that? We're-go-ing-on-the-first-sound. Nineteen Reach. Ready? Break."

When we get up there, it's not the normal cadence—it's a quick first sound. Looking at the Colt players reaction, we caught them late getting off the ball, but we were aware of what defense they were going to be in. Again, why would they change for us? They continually lined up to our strength with their strength, and on the weak side we had them outnumbered. This linebacker was over there and we were going on the first sound and he was still in the down position—these guys hadn't even raised up yet when the ball was snapped. We were split seconds ahead of them and got good angles on our blocks. They were late getting out of the gate.

Bob Talamini and Winston Hill and our halfback, Mathis or Boozer, had some beautiful blocking. Sauer, our top receiver that day, also had a major hand in blocking Lenny Lyles. Man, that first touchdown took a lot of work. I was thrilled, but not surprised. We ran the right play and caught them unprepared by using the snap count (on the first sound). There was around six minutes left in the half and now it was up to our defense to keep doing what earned them the number-one ranking in the AFL. No stopping now.

* * *

My heritage is Hungarian, and I had always heard traditional gypsy music at picnics and Hungarian church events that got my blood running. I've always been attracted to the urge to move, see what's going on, the love of life, the variety, not being tied down. I've always felt the need to continue growing, searching, discovering, learning new parts of life, new adventures. After a year in Tuscaloosa, I returned to Beaver Falls for the summer break. I was back at home, eating with Mom and hanging out with my friends, but after a week everything felt too slow and too old. I went up to the pool hall—that place would fix me, I thought. I always had a good time there. The excitement of this place used to bubble up in me like a soda can all shook up, but as I walked through those familiar doors I just felt flat. I saw the same guys bent over making amazing shots and hooting and the same guys buying beer, all smiles, but I no longer wanted to challenge somebody to a friendly game, no longer wanted to chase that high that came from making a shot under pressure. The only thing I could think of as I stood there was how much I missed being on campus back in Alabama. Beaver Falls was full of love and memories, but it was sad to stand there and grasp that I'd left without ever realizing it. This gypsy needed to move on.

I stayed around for another week and went back to Alabama early and began looking for a job. I got a tip that repossessing cars paid well and you were able to be outside, so I went and applied to GMAC and apparently they thought a big football player could handle himself, even though I had zero experience. I was stunned and amazed that they hired me.

One of the first cars we were asked to get was located in Columbus, Georgia. I had partnered up with my buddy Bobby Eli, another Yankee—but from the state of Massachusetts—who ran track for Alabama, and while we could pick 'em up and put 'em down on the field, it didn't help us cover the 180 miles to Columbus. GMAC shrugged and said they weren't responsible for transportation. Bobby thought about it for a while and suggested we just thumb it, so we went to Highway 82 and started hitchhiking our way to the car. It took us a while, and our lack of experience showed. We got a ride to the capital, Montgomery, about halfway, but the driver let us off at the edge of town at five in the morning. We asked if he knew where a truck stop was, and he pointed down an empty road. It may have been late, but it was still hot and humid as we walked down the middle of the main drag with no cars in sight. But, boy, did it ever feel exhilarating. This was new, an adventure, and neither of us complained. It took us over an hour to get through town and see the all-night lights at the truck stop. We asked around and found a ride.

When he let us off near the address we had, Bobby and I got a little nervous. Who owned the car? We doubted whoever it was would be glad to have two guys sneaking up and seemingly stealing it. Would there be an altercation?

"Should we plan a distraction?" I asked, taking the keys GMAC had given us out of my pocket. "You can do something and I can sneak in and start the car."

"Let's just see what the deal is," Bobby said. "I hope it isn't some hotheaded dude with a piece of pipe in his backseat."

We checked addresses and could tell we were getting close to the house. We began to slow down and walked next to the line of trees to stay out of sight. Then we got closer and saw the car sitting on the street.

We got in, with Bobby driving, and started back. But just outside of Selma, Alabama, an orange light flashed on the dashboard. We were not the most mechanically inclined guys attending the University so we just blew it off. Then the car started catching and making coughing noises. Again, all we had to do was get it back to Selma. No big problem.

"It's a new car, probably just a valve adjustment," I said, as if I knew anything, but I'd heard Dad talk about getting that done to his car.

"Probably," Bobby said, clearly as informed as I was. "Could be the alternator."

It began belching, and then the car started seizing. Bobby and I looked at each other.

"Not our problem," he said. "Let's just get this car dropped off." I agreed. Good plan. Three miles later the car jerked and stalled and then we just coasted, everything was dead.

We popped the hood and looked at it for about three seconds before both admitting that we had no idea what went where or how a car ran. So we slammed it shut, locked the doors, and stuck our thumbs out again. The sun was brutal, so we found a peach grove that provided shade and took turns thumbing and eating some of the juiciest peaches I've ever tasted. About forty minutes later a truck pulled over and asked us where we were headed. We told him.

"This is your lucky day, boys. I'm with Alabama's ROTC program and we're headed to Tuscaloosa to return some gear." He gestured to the back of the truck. "Hop in and I'll take you right back to campus." Bobby and I looked at each other and raced to get in the truck. Last one in is a dope! Take us back to campus?! Yes, sir. Yes, please.

GMAC never got back in contact with us about repossessing another car.

* * *

That next drive for the Colts was threatening, too. First there was a missed tackle on a swing pass to Tom Matte, which allowed him to run for thirty yards. The defense boned up and put a stop to the Colts, until finally it was fourth down and they had to try for a field goal, which they missed. But watching that over again, I don't recollect having any surprise, just relief that our defense had risen to the occasion. In fact, in my humble opinion, I think our D was the best in the game.

I had learned the dangers of being overconfident myself going into the Buffalo game earlier in the season. We were favored by about nineteen points, the same as the Colts over us in the Super Bowl. My roommate, Ray, was driving me to the airport—not just to be a pal, but because he wanted to borrow my car—and he asked me what I thought about the game. I shrugged and said, "They've got a rookie quarterback. We've got the best defense in the league. I don't see how they can score."

Well they found a way, all right. By running my interceptions back for touchdowns. I got back to New York and was trying to forget the game and my *five* picks as quickly as possible. The next morning my roommate and I were going to breakfast and Ray says, in his South Philly dialect, "Ey, I found out how they could score."

You've gotta understand that this had been after beating Kansas City, in Kansas City, two weeks prior. Man, we defeated the team that had been in the Championship Game the year before. They had been AFL champs and we beat them in their own backyard to start the season. That team had seven players on the field that day who ended up professional football Hall of Famers. So yeah, I had been feeling good about our team.

But then, two weeks later against Denver at Shea Stadium, Weeb saw the team as overconfident again. He watched as we practiced inside the stadium—instead of on the field because it was wet. He saw maybe too much relaxation. Too much horsing around and kibitzing as we ran through the motions in those cement corridors. He warned me, "We're not ready."

I looked at him and gave him a gentle elbow nudge. I mean what was he talking about? "Yeah, we're ready, Coach."

I would go on to throw another five interceptions in that game. Hard to win when you have that many turnovers.

That day hadn't started well to begin with, though. Game day morning it had been pouring cold October rain. I was riding in a limo with my dad, and the driver went onto the FDR on-ramp at 96th Street. Traffic was stopped due to a flood, and we were locked in before we even got on the FDR. For forty-five minutes we didn't move. Slowly, a single lane of traffic starting inching through the water so we finally headed to the Triborough Bridge and Shea Stadium. By the time we got to the locker room, it was empty. The guys were already dressed and out on the field—that's how late I was! In all my days of playing sports—and in every sport I'd ever played—I'd never been *that* late and the feeling was awful. Sickening. Thank God my dad was with me to confirm my story to Weeb, otherwise he never would've believed me. Hell, some of my teammates still weren't convinced I wasn't out on the town drinking or something. I mean how can you be that late? But Coach Ewbank believed the story because my father was the one who told it to him. I swear it was the flood on the FDR and even today, I'm too cautious to use the FDR to get to LaGuardia. I'll use First Avenue, Third, or Park to get uptown to 124th to get on the Triborough, but I won't use the FDR because you don't have an alternative if you get stuck. No options.

CHAPTER TEN

We got the ball back on our 20-yard line, and after a short run by Boozer, we got to one of my favorite plays of the game. Sauer and I had talked about this play on the sidelines in the second quarter. You see, I'd already hit Sauer on the quick in-route a couple of times when they came with the safety blitz. George and I decided that the next time they brought that sort of pressure, which would leave one-on-one coverage with the cornerback, we were going to run the I-go. George is going to look like he's coming in on the short in-route, I'm going to pump fake, then he's going to jump out and head upfield. And we pulled it off to perfection, which in retrospect is impressive considering it was the only time we ran that play. At home on the computer screen, I watch it again, and the execution is just beautiful, man.

Then Snell went back into action. Nine yards, then three yards. Next, it looks like I decide to take a shot downfield. With a full seven-step drop, you can see me getting my distance from the line before locking onto Maynard streaking down the right sideline with a step on his defender. I pulled the trigger and it felt like a good release, but I overshot Don by a couple of yards.

Watching the game now on my iPad, I see Don walking to the sidelines after the play. I'm surprised that I didn't realize he had left the game. I don't have a memory of Bake coming into the game right then. I swear on my mother's grave I do not remember the next play. I'm stunned to see it.

This is crazy.

We were strong-formation left, and they brought the free safety on a blitz to our offensive right side. Bake Turner, now playing as a split end on our right, having taken Maynard's place, reads the blitz beautifully and runs his adjusted I-route, which was a slant in-route to the inside. I read the blitz and ended up throwing the ball to Bake, just like we had it drawn up for that situation.

But it was a lousy throw.

It headed in the right direction, but I threw the ball way too low and it bounced in front of him. I sincerely do not remember that play. I can't wait to see Bake again and apologize. That was my bad. There was only one guy in the secondary between him and the goal line. If I had made the pass on the money instead of into the dirt, Bake would still be running. He'd would have juked the DB and gone in for a touchdown. Man, I'm disappointed in myself.

Good thing we won. You make a play or a pass like that and lose the game then those thoughts don't go away. Ever. I'd have remembered that for sure. Sometimes it goes the other way, too. Once, before a practice, we were watching film of a previous game in which we came out on top. I was with the offense, and when guys made good plays in the game, it got recognition from the players and the coaches.

We were watching and I threw a strike to Maynard, who had run a post pattern, hitting him perfectly midstride. He ran for a touchdown. A beautiful play.

"Helluva throw, Joe!"

Everybody was admiring it. The offensive line did their job and gave me time to set up and throw. Maynard had beat his man. Pete Lammons, our tight end, also beat his man and was open running a twelve-yard curl in.

"Wait a second, Coach, run that back," I say.

This was clearly not my rookie season because I had enough confidence to own up to what really happened. Coach runs it back and we watch the perfect pass again. We run it back again and I point out: "Look at Lammons, fellas. I was going to Pete!"

Groans from the players and coaches.

"But I'm happy with the results." It worked out. Everybody did their job on the play, and I got away with a high pass that was on time. Kind of the opposite of the low pass to Bake.

They show Weeb pacing the sidelines shortly after, and that brings a smile to my face. Look at him, with those pants rolled up and that Jets hat snug on top of his head. We called him Weeb when talking about him, and he didn't mind it if you did that to his face, either, but I'd usually just call him Coach.

They cut to the next play, and I remember it because it was a great opportunity. If George and I were on the same page as we normally were, then it would have made for a positive play. But George and I weren't, so I had to eat it. The Colts brought another safety blitz and I couldn't find him. Even after stepping up in the pocket, I was taken down for what I believe was the one time I got tackled in that game while carrying the ball. Seeing it now, it still stings— it led to fourth down, and ultimately a missed field goal, that just happened to be kicked into a twenty-mile-per-hour crosswind.

On the sidelines, I asked George what happened and he said he ran the I-go and I had stuck with the I-read and never saw him. Basically, it was my fault. I hadn't thought about running the I-go, thinking we were reverting back to the regular I pattern. Again, my bad.

Then the Colts come back with a big play, a fifty-eight yard rush by Tom Matte, which got them all the way down to our 16-yard line. Matte put a good move on our strong safety, Jim Hudson, to break free for the long run. Free safety Billy Baird was able to get a hand on Matte's ankle to trip him up. Sample put the finishing touch on the tackle, which Matte thought was late. Matte jumped up, angry, and got in Johnny's face, but Sample doesn't back down in the least. The two of them are face-to-face, jawing with one another. I love Johnny's attitude.

After a short run by Colt fullback Hill, Morrall tries a pass to WR Willie Richardson, who's running a post route. Sample read it beautifully to make the interception.

* * *

I went to Alabama to play ball and had hopes that I could someday work as a pro; however, I did have a backup plan, too, in case my dreams didn't come true: become a school-teacher and coach. Originally, business was something I thought I might be good at. I liked numbers, all right. But they told me my grades weren't good enough for the School of Commerce. That my boards didn't measure up, either. Hoping to keep me eligible to play, they enrolled me in the School of Education.

With that decided, and football under way, I could turn some of my energy toward the Southern Belles on campus. When I got to Tuscaloosa, I didn't have a steady girl. Then, after the Auburn game my freshman year, this real pretty girl came up to me and started a conversation. We hit it off—turned out a teammate was seeing her friend, so we started partaking in some decidedly risky business. Alabama dorms at the time, well, they were absolutely, strictly not coed. But, come on. Think that was going to stop us? Besides, the girls lived on the first floor. Piece of cake.

He and I would walk over to their building and sneak in through their windows. If we got caught, we'd have been kicked out of college, not to mention getting booted from the football team. But sometimes, risks must be taken in life. We'd sit in the room, we'd kiss. We had a lot of fun. Even if getting caught was never far from our minds. The added edge of danger just made it that much more exciting. We had a tight schedule as my teammate and I had to get back to our dorm before our eleven p.m. curfew.

That relationship got tougher in my junior year, because there were more girls, and my gypsy eyes wandered. But that goes both ways and I can remember going to meet her and seeing her outside her dormitory talking to a guy. Man, that was an ugly, unfamiliar feeling and my insides were turning and my chest burned with anger. But, what right did I have? I talked to other girls. It was the first time I really felt jealousy and it stayed with me. I left and went back to my dorm and gave it a lot of thought. What were our expectations with each other? I wasn't ready to be true to her. What do you do when you feel so strongly about somebody, but aren't sure of the next level of commitment?

She had come back to school for a fifth year. I got drafted and by the end of my senior year, I was getting ready to move to New York. But I wasn't being clear with her and she wasn't sure what was going on, either, so she confronted me. She wanted clarity, and that was fair. She asked me bluntly what we were going to do. And I told her. I can remember telling her. We were standing face-to-face outside of her dorm and I said: I'm leaving. I told her I loved her, and I did, but I wasn't ready to make a move and get on track to get married. I wanted the love affair to go on, but I had to be truthful. I had to go on living and I wasn't sure what was going to happen once I moved to New York and started playing for the Jets. That was my reality, but maybe it came out as an excuse.

"Look, I've got a job," I said. "I have to go make that work. That's my top priority. I don't even have an apartment yet. I don't know what to expect. I can't take you with me to New York."

Looking back, I wasn't in the kind of love that you need to be in to make that kind of commitment.

And there were tears, from both of us. We were standing right out in front of her dorm on the sidewalk talking about it. I just felt awful. I felt the pain she was going through. She didn't want it to end and wanted me to take her to New York, but I had to be truthful with her.

I did move to New York and got to work. Four years after that, here we are competing in the Super Bowl, so work has been good. And a lot of that has to do with a man named Matt Snell.

* * *

Man, Snell was a beast in that game. We got back out on the field, and it was great to see Matt doing what he did best. All that running he did and he still wanted more. So I kept giving it to him, even if his next three runs failed to get us a first down.

It's fourth-and-5, so I watched Curley Johnson come in to kick. He was our punter, a backup halfback, a backup full-back, a backup tight end, a backup wide receiver. And he was an all-star when it came to comedy. In the locker room, on the buses, standing in the hotel, heck, even on the side-lines, Curley was always dropping something in his Texas drawl that would have you bent over laughing. Championship rings aside—Curley should have gotten something for being the funniest guy on that Jets team.

I watch as Paul Crane makes a perfect long snap to Curley in our end zone, and seeing how close they were to blocking that punt gives me a negative thrill, man. But Curley always seemed to find a way to get things done, and he managed to get the ball off.

I then remind myself, looking out my window at the Loxahatchee River, that there are twenty-two players on the football field and the game is often decided by who beats themselves. The team that makes the most mistakes usually loses, and that's true at any level and any sport. Earl wasn't throwing strikes all day and neither was I.

With that in mind, I hit play and the broadcast resumes with a short pass to the Colts' Jerry Hill. Then, after a time-out and on second-and-9, the Colts pulled a trick play out of their hat and tried a flea flicker! This particular play was scrutinized and discussed extensively over the years because wide receiver Jimmy Orr broke free behind the left side of our defense. He was wide open and standing alone waving his hands over his head. But Morrall didn't see him and threw down the right hash mark to running back Jerry Hill instead. Hud, our strong safety, read the play. He had eyes on Morrall and undercut the throw, and came up with the ball when the whistle blew. Interception number three for the day.

That's their last play before halftime—before Mr. Bob Hope takes the field. Seeing him on that screen now, I can't help but remember the few times we crossed paths. He asked that I call him "Bob," but I mean, come on—he's Mr. Hope! I could never just call him Bob.

Mr. Hope graciously invited me to do some of his shows over the years and on such an occasion he taught me one of the most valuable lessons I've learned in my life. I was backstage when I asked somebody where he was.

I was told, "Mr. Hope is taking a nap."

A nap?

Twenty minutes later, he walked out looking darn perky and alert.

"You take naps, Mr. Hope?"

"Let me tell you, Joe..." He broke down the not-so-secret truth of only taking twenty-minute naps. Any longer than that and you can wake up all fogged in the head, and it's as if you're fighting grogginess. I meditate, too, but naps became a vital part of my daily schedule from that point forward. I still set an alarm for twenty-seven minutes—a few minutes to fall asleep—and I wake up ready to go give a talk or throw a football with my grandson or help my daughter with her family ancestry research or sit up and watch an old Championship Game I haven't really analyzed in fifty years.

Bob Hope was massive back then, and it's jarring in comparison to today how quickly they interview him. Nowadays he'd have given a routine and they'd have some popular singer or band on a temporary stage. Not just popular—the most popular. Someone like Elvis, who I met for the first time in '69. In fact, Elvis goes back to my childhood in the 1950s, following my older brother Bob who, at sixteen or so, was nine years older than me. He was smooth, had pegged pants, and I'd grown up watching him combing his hair back and putting on cologne and just getting slick. Elvis Presley was huge and I could see the influence he had on my bigger brothers.

To his credit, my brother Bob had style, too. And he wasn't just a bit of a player—he was dedicated! As soon as Bob turned sixteen and got legit, he quit school. I remember watching him come home and seeing the foundry dust from his job at the Mayer China factory on him. Because of that, I always looked on the bottom of plates and cups just out of habit to see where they were made. When I was a sophomore in college and we were in Knoxville to play the University of Tennessee, at the pregame meal I flipped over a plate and sure enough—there it was: Mayer China, Beaver Falls, PA. I passed it around to my teammates, who really didn't care all that much.

I always saw Bob get all primed for going out. One time I followed him and his group of buddies as they walked down Seventh Avenue, the town's main drag. He went into Earl's Dairy, which was in between a couple of movie houses. I'd have to stay low because I would always go over there and get sent back home. Bob would see me, and naturally he didn't want his little brother around. I walked in, though, and saw the soda fountains and the cold cuts for sandwiches in the refrigerated display case. In the back, there was an area with a jukebox and a pinball machine and a couple tables off to the right where Bob and his friends were hanging out.

Bob did have to babysit, but it wasn't like he ever took me into Earl's Dairy—I had followed strictly out of interest. I learned a lot from Bob, like how to throw a football from the ear. And his buddy Doodles taught me the MF word when he yelled it with such emphasis after spotting an impressive spider down at the river.

Well, we all know how much punch those kinds of words can have for a six-year-old. So I used it as soon as possible—and that just happened to be when my mother, Mrs. Knapp, and the Filipilli sisters were there on our front porch relaxing, talking about the day. I was sitting on the steps daydreaming and I remembered the excitement of how Doodles had said it, so I blurted it out. I had no idea what I was saying, but there was a long silence on that porch with four ladies looking at me. I said it again and my mom simply looked over at me and, without raising her voice or changing her cadence, said, "Joey, don't say that."

And even afterward, Bob was still occasionally detailed with looking after me. But on this occasion, I followed him into Earl's Dairy and snuck around into the back area hoping he wouldn't notice me. Just then I heard it. This music from the jukebox. Music that was like nothing I'd ever come across before. Elvis Presley was singing "Blue Suede Shoes." That might have been the first time I was aware that I liked music. I grew to love it so much that I'd take my little radio into the locker room at the University of Alabama to get my juices flowing for practice. I needed music, needed to be in tune.

But the first time I tried to use my radio as a rookie with the Jets on a game day, it didn't go over too well. Some of the older guys didn't share my taste. There was no music in the locker room. Before one of the first games that I was going to play, though, I was getting dressed. The offensive linemen sat across from the quarterbacks and receivers and the defensive people were in another area. So I was across from Dave Herman, who the veterans called "Haystack" or "Stack" because he was somewhat of a country bumpkin. He was an older guy who was just fired up all the time.

I took my radio out, turned it on, and instantly he shouted, "Turn that goddamn thing down!"

I was startled and, boy, he put some heat on that instruction and I didn't waste any time doing as he asked. I turned it down, but not off because I still had to feel it.

But when I was able to put tunes on, I almost always did. In fact, after I started going to Vegas, I always did my best to try and catch some music, Tom Jones, Johnny Mathis, Harry Belafonte, Wayne Newton, and Elvis's shows. I'd go see Don Rickles perform and when he caught me in the audience—man, did that get embarrassing. I got to know Don, which was wonderful, but if he saw you during his show, watch out! He'd say something nice and then do his bit where he turns and calls you a schmuck in front of everybody. He beat us all up.

Vegas felt good, though. Food was good, winning at the tables felt good, and the golf was wonderful. I'd stay at the Desert Inn. The rumor was that the famous recluse Howard Hughes lived upstairs. Never met him, but when we'd walk out to the golf course, we'd peek up and it was good fun to try and see the mysterious Mr. Hughes.

The first time I went to an Elvis show, though, I was blown away. He isn't called the King for nothing. The ladies were screaming and the energy was electric. After that first concert, I was able to meet him and was stunned that he was a football fan. When we walked into his dressing room, he stood up and he was close in height to me, a good-sized guy, and lean at that show. He knew my name, which floored me. I never expected him to recognize me, although I quickly discovered that he was an inquisitive fellow and wanted to know about my sport and asked all sorts of questions.

I was absolutely starstruck, of course. Then, on another trip to Vegas, I took my dad to see Elvis perform, and we went backstage after another amazing show. He just really knocked you back with how powerful he was on that stage. So much presence. He was wearing white with a high collar around his neck this time and dropping in some karate moves while he sang. Once again, he welcomed us in and was the most gracious man.

We shook hands, and he was all "Joe, how's it going," but when he talked to my dad, he called him Mr. Namath. He put his arm around my father and walked him over to the couch in the dressing room, and the two of them sat down and talked. I didn't even really converse with him that time—he was over there across the room with Dad. Elvis had respect. He was a gentleman.

I've always admired the artists that I've known. Whether they're musicians, actors, singers, dancers, or painters, they have the passion to succeed and work hard enough to try and become their best. They understand how hard it is to get to a high level of expertise, both through dedication and luck. We can all benefit from having a passion and the drive to excel.

CHAPTER ELEVEN

As a kid, my buddies and I watched the Beaver Falls High School football games, and during halftime, ten or fifteen of us would run out onto the empty side field behind the bleachers and play what we called free-for-all. No one picked teams—somebody simply threw a crushed paper cup into the air and we all scrambled for it. Whoever grabbed it just started running while everybody else tried to take him down.

Halftimes at Super Bowls are very different. As a player, you have to prepare for the extra-long break. As a team, you have to practice taking that long a breather. The standard twelve minutes that starts when you get into the lockers stretches out to over half an hour. Some players change uniforms and have a nutritional snack while they're waiting to go back on the field. Our game even had a little longer halftime break. I remember watching the previous year's World Championship from the stands and wondering when the floats and marching bands were going to end and the football would start again.

The broadcast I've been watching doesn't show much by way of halftime festivities compared to today, but I don't need that to trigger memories of how antsy and eager we all were to get back out there. To pass the time, some of the guys went to their lockers and dug around for their coffin sticks and then headed to the shower room area to smoke. Hey, it was the '60s! We didn't know any better. The only off-limits areas were the locker and training rooms. And if you're curious who was smoking, I'll tell you it'd be easier to name all the players who weren't.

I had quit by 1967. Up till then, I smoked before and after practice and at halftime. Of course, smoking then was not considered dangerous or addictive. I mean, that was the first thing at halftime; the guys that needed it went right for their packs after they came in and met with their coaches, who smoked, too! We didn't know it was bad. I was getting recruited in the winter of 1961, when I was seventeen, and I went to the Pittsburgh airport and as I was walking through the door there was a guy handing out free four-pack packages of cigarettes. He was just giving them to everybody walking past. They knew what they were doing. It was just normal in sports. I remember always noticing people's yellow, nicotine-stained fingers.

After I quit, I wouldn't date a girl who smoked. I couldn't stand that smell up close any longer. And also, I hate to judge people, but for somebody who didn't learn by the time we knew how deadly the habit was—well, I'd have to be really drinking to be able to overlook that. And yes, I understand the irony in that last sentence, but while I was drinking, I could come up with all sorts of screwball reasoning to do just about anything.

Meantime, I still thought it was fine to chew tobacco. I just didn't realize how detrimental it was for those of us addicted to it. I dipped snuff for around twenty years—until my daughter Jessica and I made a deal that she'd stop sucking her thumb if I'd stop chewing tobacco. And we did. Growing up, we were forbidden from smoking, and Dad, who smoked at the time, by the way, felt strongly about it. A kid had reported that he saw me and my friends with cigarettes, which was partially true. We had seen an older boy with smokes, and I snatched the pack out of his hands, and Linwood, my buddy Tony, and I began playing a game of keep-away with this guy. Well, he got back at us and said something to my dad. How that turned into smoking is a stretch, but Dad heard my name and cigarettes and did some sort of parental math. So when I got home it was straight to the cellar, no questions asked, for a beating with the belt.

Drinking and smoking were just part of the game, part of life back then. In 1967, I was spending the offseason in an apartment at the Palm Bay Club in Miami. I was having dinner with my mom and some horse-racing royalty when I pulled out a coffin nail. Liz Whitney Tippett was at the head of the table and saw me lighting up. She said, "Namath! What are you doing? You're an athlete! You shouldn't smoke!"

"I'm going to quit right before we go into training camp this summer."

"That's bull!"

My mom also smoked, and naturally had one in her hand. Mrs. Tippett looked at her and said, "Rose, you should quit, too."

"Oh, I'll quit when Joey quits."

I looked at my mother and said, "What'd you just say?"

"Oh, honey, I'll quit when you quit."

I had planned on quitting, but this was now a challenge. I took out my pack and crumpled it up and dropped it on the table.

Connie Dinkler, the owner of the club with her husband, took out her pack and said, "Wait, wait! I want to quit, too. Let's make a bet!"

She took a napkin and wrote an agreement stating the first person to smoke in the next five years would owe the other ten thousand dollars. I thought, dang, that's twice as much as my dad makes in a year! No way I'm losing that! She framed it and put it on the wall of the club. No way either one of us could cheat, since we were living on the club grounds.

I stopped until filming a TV show called *The Waverly Wonders* in 1978. Bored, I bummed a smoke from somebody during a long break. I then bought a pack while driving home. The next day I had a pounding headache, and as I reached for my smokes in my pocket, I paused and the realization hit that it was the damn cigarettes. That was the end of my smoking.

The drinking was what would kick my butt for a long time. I believe any of us can be brought to our knees whether from physical or emotional pain. Over the years, I learned how fragile we humans can be. Emotionally, I used that as an excuse to start drinking again. Having my daughters and going through a divorce and just the aching from the family being split apart caused me so much hurt. It was difficult, so I drank.

I would drink all day sometimes. If I had a flight, I'd be at the airport an hour early drinking a salty dog or whatever. It was a nasty habit, and that's why I am thankful for the experience with Suzy Kolber live on national TV. I didn't recognize the problem myself at the time, but this made it undeniable. She interviewed me on the sidelines during halftime at a 2003 Jets game. It was a Monday Night Football broadcast and I'd somehow managed to end up there alone, without either Jessica or Jimmy to keep an eye on me. I had been drinking since the morning, was drunk, and said I wanted to kiss her while we were filming the segment.

That night I was still drunk and didn't realize what I had done, but the next morning, my best friend in the world, Jimmy Walsh, called and alerted me to what had happened. I asked him if he could try and get Suzy's number and for permission to contact her. I wanted to apologize. I had embarrassed and disrespected her on national TV and it was not fair to have put her in that position. I never saw the clip, but I called her and asked for understanding and forgiveness. You don't treat people like that, and I apologized. She was beyond gracious. She was so good at accepting what had transpired and letting me know that she understood I made a mistake and didn't beat me over the head with it. She accepted the apology with wonderful form. I saw it as a blessing in disguise.

I had embarrassed my friends and family and could not escape that feeling. I haven't had a drink since. That shame is where I found my strength to deal with the addiction. With the help of my recovery I learned that I had used my divorce as an excuse to go back to drinking. That knowledge made me a stronger individual.

But, you know, I started drinking regularly because of a literal PIA during my rookie year. When I was playing, if you had a problem with pain, you'd simply try to block it out mentally, and if you couldn't, well, then you'd get an injection or take pills. For some, it was Percocet. Others dulled it with alcohol. On most Tuesdays or Wednesdays you might get an injection. We never knew and never asked what was in those shots, except that after a day I was able to move around again. Aspirating, draining the knees, was common. What we now refer to as a TBI, a traumatic brain injury, was just getting your bell rung. That was fixed by cracking some smelling salts under your nose. Cut right through that fog.

One game, the Boston Patriots got me with a safety blitz and a knee to my butt that caused a painful ugly bruise right on my hind side. I couldn't even sit down! I had no idea what to do for the aching, so I called Joe Hirsch, my older, wiser roommate in New York. He was a brilliant sportswriter and a leading horse-racing columnist. He said something to the effect of "that's what Scotch is for."

And he was right. The Scotch did take away the pain. At least until I got hit again. And then the extra pads helped until it was the Scotch's turn again and the cycle just kept going.

During one game against the Kansas City Chiefs, I got hit in the head, saw *a flash of gold*, and was knocked down. My center, John Schmitt, helped me up. I staggered around for a few seconds then walked toward the Chiefs' huddle. I put a hand on a player's shoulder and said, "I don't know which one of you so-and-sos hit me, but it was a damn good lick." Then I turned around and went back to my huddle. Absolutely zero recollection of what happened after that.

Then there are times you get hit so damn hard, you don't know how long you're down, or how long you lost consciousness. I took a major blow against the Raiders once and I can remember a tingling sensation in my arms. I got off the field with some help, but I still returned to the game and played. In medical books, I sometimes see mTBI, meaning "mild" traumatic brain injury. I'm confused as to how "mild" and "traumatic" go together. There were many times in my pro career when I got hit in the head or my head whiplashed into the turf and I got up feeling a little dizzy. I'd close my eyes and hold my head. After a few uncertain steps, I'd recover my bearings and go back in the huddle, ready to play.

But during a game in Denver, I took the best hit of my career. Dave Costa, a defensive tackle from the Broncos, got me right in the solar plexus with his helmet and drove me into the ground. It was a beautiful shot. Clean. I had just released the ball and while my right arm was extended, Costa left the ground about two yards ahead of me and drove his helmet into my stomach. It was a dead-center shot. Not only did he knock every bit of wind out of me, but he also slammed my body down with such force that I got whiplash as my head crashed into the turf.

What pissed me off was the crowd reaction. I was on the ground, my arms splayed out—looking about half-past dead. Maybe I was blacked out, but the first thing I recall was hearing the fans. Dr. Nicholas and the trainers came out to attend to me. They didn't move my neck in case something was damaged, but they tried to get some air back into me. I felt the sting of smelling salts as somebody cracked one under my nose and I heard the cheering.

I wanted to shut those fans up. We called a time-out so I'd have a moment to collect myself. I refused to leave the game. I wasn't even playing the Broncos anymore. I was playing the fans. Knowing Denver would never expect me to drop back for a pass again on the very next play, that's exactly what I did. And hit Bake Turner on a post corner route that turned into a long gainer, setting up our score that followed.

After the game, the media asked me about the fans cheering. I was mad and said, "I bet they wouldn't be cheering if it was one of their own kids lying out on the field." That was the first time I heard cheering—happiness—that I was down and hurt.

But the hit? Perfection.

Dave came into the visitors' locker room after the game and asked me how I was doing.

I said, "Fine. But man, that *was* a helluva hit!"

We all knew it. When, as a team, we watched the highlights, I had to marvel at what a perfect hit he'd landed on me. Costa bent me in half.

To be clear though, the Scotch that I drank to dull the pain in my rear end was not my first sip of alcohol— although I didn't drink much in college. I might have a beer at a fraternity party, and once on spring break, someone injected vodka into a watermelon that we ate. Maybe even more than one spring break. Even at Alabama, though, I still hadn't lost my boyhood tendency to push things a little too far sometimes. I lived in the athletic dormitory, and the coaches came in and checked on us every night after curfew. There were a lot of rules, but one was absolute: No drinking during the season. When you're away from home and on a team with guys three years older than you, hanging out at parties...well, it was common to have a few beers with your buddies on the weekend. When I wanted to act adult, I ordered a Seven and Seven (Seagram's Seven Crown whiskey and 7 Up soda). No, I never got downright drunk in Tuscaloosa, but I wasn't afraid of a drink or two.

I should have been, though. The weekend of December 7, 1963, we had a free week after our 10–8 loss to Auburn. Our next game was originally scheduled for Friday against Miami. President John F. Kennedy was assassinated on November 22, and the annual Army–Navy game was pushed back to December 7, pushing back our game against Miami to a week later.

Well that weekend a businessman told Coach that he saw me and another player downtown drunk and directing traffic from the middle of the street. The following Monday Coach Bryant found me in the athletic dormitory eating lunch.

"Joe, come on." He nodded in a direction away from anybody else. "I want to talk with you."

We walked into one of the guest rooms on the dormitory's first floor, a small room with one bed in it. We were standing there and he was clearly unhappy. "I got word from someone downtown. I know him. He's a businessman. I know you and I know you'll tell me the truth. So, I am going to ask you: Were you downtown, drunk? This fella said you were drunk and directing traffic."

"No sir, that's not true," I said, in disbelief. I knew what he was talking about. I had been downtown and in the middle of an intersection.

"I was downtown, but I was with a friend and we were

pushing his car out of the intersection. It was our equipment manager Hoot Owl Hicks's car, you know, his old beater? It broke down right in the middle of the intersection. We were pushing it out of the way."

Coach Bryant stopped. It made sense to him and I could tell he was relieved and believed me. "Okay, good."

Then he added, "Did you have anything to drink Saturday?"

Again, team rules forbid any players from drinking, but I wasn't going to lie to Coach. I didn't get drunk on Saturday, I hadn't even touched a drink when we were pushing the car out of the intersection. I had gone to a fraternity party though, and had one Seven and Seven.

"Yes, sir, I had a drink Saturday night."

Coach Bryant looked at me and I watched his eyes close. "Ohhhh." He groaned loudly and fell back onto the bed. I honestly thought he was having a heart attack.

"Coach! Coach! Are you all right?"

He mumbled, "Yeah, yeah" but remained motionless on the bed, eyes still closed.

He lay in silence for one of those minutes that seems like an hour. He slowly stood up and said, "I think I'm going to have to suspend you."

I stood there, stunned.

He looked at his watch and said, "Come over to my office at one-fifteen."

At one-ten, I walked into the coaches' office, unsure of where my college football career was going. I waited outside in the foyer. All of the assistant coaches were standing off to the side talking.

Coach Bryant opened the door and the conversations ended. He came out, walked over to me, and said, "Well, we had a meeting and a lot of coaches feel like I should just punish you some way here on campus and not suspend you. We could punish you some other way, but you broke a rule and I am going to have to suspend you. If I don't suspend you, then I will retire after this year, because it's going against what I believe."

"No, sir. I don't want you to retire."

Looking back, I think he said what he said as much to the coaches in the room as to me. Coach Bryant looked at me and gestured to start walking out of the room. "Okay, I will tell you what we are going to do," he said, as we walked together out of the office and across the parking lot. "Joe, if you don't want to stay here anymore, and do things the way I want you to do them, I can get you in someplace else. If there's another school you want to go to, I'll try and get you in there."

I stammered, completely and emotionally blown out—he was talking about transferring me. "No. No, sir. I don't want to go anywhere else. I want to stay here."

"Okay, this is what you have to do," he said. "We'll move you out of the athletic dorm and find another place to live. You'll attend every one of your classes and be a damn good citizen. And, if you do that—"

I waited. I knew what was going to happen—I was back on the team!

"—then you can come back and try out for the football team in the spring."

Holy smokes—I had been kicked off the team.

When I had been fielding college offers, one of them broke the rules and offered me six thousand dollars and a new car to play for them. I mentioned it to my brother

Sonny, who simply said, "You want to play for a bunch of cheaters?"

I didn't, so I made arrangements to move out of the athletic dorm and into a student room in Petty Hall with a fellow Pennsylvanian, Timmy Thompson, who was on a baseball scholarship. His place wouldn't be available for a few days, though, and I was left homeless. Somehow word got around and Mary Harmon, Coach Bryant's wife, invited me to sleep in the basement of their home.

I missed our last two games of my junior season—against Miami and Ole Miss in the Sugar Bowl. Both were won by us on national television. It's a special kind of hurt, being isolated from teammates, imagining the adrenaline and joy and camaraderie as they played and thankfully won. Steve Sloan, a sophomore, and Jack Hurlbut, a senior, took over the quarterbacking.

I was, meanwhile, with my buddy Mike Bite at his house in Birmingham, and we watched the Alabama–Miami game. We jumped out to a 17–0 lead, but they rallied in the fourth quarter to make the score 17–12. I was terrified. As a first-teamer, I felt personally responsible when Alabama couldn't advance the ball and had to punt it back to Miami. But our linebacker Jackie Sherrill intercepted a Miami pass to end their last scoring threat as we won the game.

Hoot Owl, my buddy Frankie C., and I drove to watch the Sugar Bowl in New Orleans. I'm surprised Hoot's jalopy—the same one I pushed out of the intersection—made it that far. Since I was no longer on the team, on campus, or even in the state of Alabama, technically, in my mind, I wouldn't be breaking any rules if I drank. And it was New Year's Eve in New Orleans, so I may have had a drink or two. We beat

Ole Miss 12–7 in the Sugar Bowl as Tim Davis kicked four field goals.

The suspension hurt—and it should have. I broke the rules and I wasn't the one who got to decide if it was a little or a big misstep—nobody made me take a drink. I accepted Coach's punishment and knew it set an example. But there was a time before that when I saw a similar experience unravel in front of me.

A few months before my suspension, Coach Bryant called a team meeting after practice. The rules had been set: You needed to be at team meetings ahead of time. You couldn't take a chance on being one minute late, so five really meant four fifty-five. Coach started talking, officially starting the meeting, and my roommate, Butch Henry, a senior from Selma, Alabama, opened the door just a crack and tried to slide into the room unnoticed.

Coach saw, paused, stared at him in front of the quiet room, and said, "Get outta here. You're late."

Butch tried to explain. "Coach, I was in the trainer's room getting worked on. We—"

Coach Bryant cut him off. "Hell, son, I don't care if you were in church. You are late. Get outta here. We don't need you."

Butch left and Coach Bryant continued the meeting.

The whole team knew how respectful and dedicated Butch was and also how badly he'd injured his knee. He was a senior and one of our team leaders. Butch left the meeting and got straight into his car and began driving home to Selma. He told me later that when he got halfway there, around Centerville, he stopped, thought things over, and decided to turn back and meet with Coach Bryant. He knew Coach was strict with rules, but that he was also not in the wrong. They met, worked it out, and Butch was back next practice.

But unlike Butch, I *was* in the wrong and had done this to myself. But I never had a problem with my dealing with Coach—if given the chance again, I would still choose to tell the truth rather than look into his eyes and lie.

So, I got suspended for not really drinking, but, man, was that a harbinger for things to come. I was always boozing at night with the Jets. Even at training camp, we'd finish up and go to a bar and have a beer or two to swish out the cottonmouth. That's what we all thought, for real. I learned that technique from the veterans, the same ones who chain-smoked at halftime.

Later on, when I'd retired from pro ball and my daughter Jessica was around two years old, my wife, Deborah, asked me to stop drinking. We were living in LA and she wanted me to go get help at an inpatient facility—a request that surprised and scared me. I didn't think I had a problem and assumed I could stop anytime that I wanted to. But I knew she was right enough for me to agree to see a psychologist in Brentwood. I'd go talk to him about why I was drinking, and then I'd leave that session and stop at a liquor store on the way home and buy a pint of vodka.

I thought I could get away with that, but she could smell it. While going through her agony of me being deceptive with her, she asked again if I would be willing to check into a facility. I had gone to get guidance and help, but I wasn't accepting of it and let her down, so I had to prove that I didn't have a problem. I was embarrassed to think I couldn't stop on my own. I had to prove that I was in control to myself so I promised her that I would quit. That worked for thirteen years until the divorce, when Slick gave me an excuse to start drinking again. Who is Slick? That's the voice in my head, always talking about "What's so bad about one glass of wine at dinner? You can control this—you haven't drank in so long. Red wine is good for you!" Every now and then Slick whispers, but having a name for him makes me listen to him differently. And, health-wise, I'd probably be dead by now if I hadn't stopped drinking.

* * *

There were no voices of doubt in our heads during halftime in 1969, but we knew the game was far from over. It was an upbeat, energetic Jets locker room, the exact opposite of what I imagined the Colts locker room to be. We were just thinking positive things. We were poised and confident, looking forward to the second half.

Locker rooms for pro football teams are a unique setting, unlike anything else I've experienced in life. You have a group of men, some close buddies, some who rub the others the wrong way, racism on both sides, all packed together with adrenaline, joy, depression, camaraderie, and anger, all swirling around depending on a variety of cir-cumstances. It's like a pressurized microcosm of society. Coming in on a Monday after a lousy performance the day before was humbling, awful. Knowing that I had cost the team a win was a lonely feeling. The one thing about a locker room in sports, though, is that winning cures every-thing. There's a beautiful feeling of elation that comes from competing together as a team in a violent physical contest and coming out on top.

The locker rooms weren't my favorite places to hang, though, when I was on the Jets—that would have been the night spots I frequented at a pace that just seems exhausting in hindsight. But maybe the clubs and the locker rooms weren't all that different for us Jets—at least when it came to what we mostly talked about in either place: The Ladies.

And I still remember the gal that started it all. It was junior high in the eighth grade when she just took my identification bracelet. I was damn proud of it—a piece of jewelry! This one was not gold, like the bracelets I'd wear later. It was plain metal, a terrific birthday gift from my mother. But I didn't even know what that meant, to give a girl a bracelet with my name on it. Why is she taking my identification? She just comes up to me in the common area, smiles, and starts talking as she takes my hand and slides the bracelet right off and onto her wrist. I guess that meant she was my girlfriend? I wasn't exactly sure.

We went to a school dance together and I walked her home. I was holding her hand, feeling all warm inside, when we got to her doorstep. She leaned in, and like some gravitational pull that was impossible to resist, I leaned in, too, and we kissed. The softness of her lips was amazing. I swear to God, I had never felt that. I mean my mom kissed me good-bye, and my dad always gave me a smooch on the forehead, but that kiss on the lips was something that altered my life.

And you can bet I went chasing similar experiences after that. Even fifteen years later, I still went out looking for the company of a lady. I would go to practice, come home, finish my football homework, maybe grab a meal with some buddies, and then hit some clubs. There was nothing better than the nightlife in New York City. I thrived on the energy, the variety, the unpredictable nature of what might happen. Jack Lambert—not the Pittsburgh Steelers linebacker with the same name—owned the Pussycat. The ribs were outstanding, but maybe the fact that Playboy Bunnies frequented the place had something to do with attracting a crowd.

My building in New York, the Newport East, was home to the owners of some of the hottest places in the city to spend your late nights: Barry Skolnick ran a fun place called the Golden Twenties, and a guy who would become one of my closest friends, Bobby Van, had Dudes 'n Dolls and the Jet Set. During those first couple of years in New York, I didn't just become friends with them, I became a regular patron of their establishments.

Eventually, me, Bobby Van, and another buddy figured that if we were going to be doing all that, we might as well go out to our own place. And at that time in 1968, I was hardly at my address except to use the bed. I don't remember making a single meal at home the entire time I was living in New York.

The other buddy was Ray Abruzzese, a South Philly native and a teammate from both Alabama and the Jets. I met Ray at Tuscaloosa when he was a senior under Coach Bryant and I was a freshman. Ray was twenty-four when he was a senior, much older than his classmates, and one story goes that a professor asked him a question and he shook his head silently. A few minutes later the professor asked him a similar question.

"Hey, I told ya I didn't know," Ray said. "I'll let you know when I know the answer. Don't bother me. I'll talk to you after class."

That's the honest-to-God story. Ray was not at the University of Alabama for an education. He was up-front. He went to Hines Junior College in Mississippi before transferring to Alabama to play as a defensive back and halfback. He was the oldest guy on the team, and we had some fun. I think the coaches may have asked him to help me out, but all he helped me out of was study hall.

We played pro ball together on the Jets in 1965 and 1966 before he retired. While in New York, Ray lived with me for a bit, too. One day, in fact, Dick Schaap and sportscaster Howard Cosell stopped by to see me. We sat in the living room and talked—although Howard was doing most of the talking—while Ray was asleep in his bedroom. Suddenly, Ray comes stumbling out of his room in his T-shirt and boxer shorts, walks toward the television set, and does a double-take when he sees Cosell. Ray said, "Oh, Howard! I thought you were on television. I was just coming out to turn you off."

Dick and I roared with laughter, but Ray's line seemed to stun Howard for about fifteen seconds until he came to and unleashed every derogatory term for an Italian he knew.

When we were at the height of our carousing, Ray wasn't with the Jets anymore, but he and I were moving around together. He was working at Dudes 'n Dolls, Bobby Van's club. Bobby's given name was Bobby Vannuchi. We were three bachelors, so the club we opened was named Bachelors III. The three of us put it together financially. We were the owners. Bobby got the managers, but all three of us walked the streets looking for locations. Bobby would find some address and we'd go there and then just start walking around looking for spaces. We found a place on the west side of Lexington Avenue between 61st and 62nd Streets.

The spot was an immediate success, with lines outside. I really enjoyed meeting the people who came in. Janis Joplin was one of my favorites. She was a hell-raiser, boy. But she was always just shining, this wave of energy coming from her. Paul Anka and Tom Jones and players from other teams would roll in. Howard Cosell would bring in OJ Simpson. Dick Cavett, too. One time Bing Crosby, who was on his way to Europe, decided to drop by before boarding the ship that was taking him there.

Bobby, Ray, and I were such good friends that I don't think we ever signed a contract when we agreed to open Bachelors III. Everything was good on a handshake.

This was the summer of 1967 going into the 1968 season and sure, I was going there most nights. I might have dinner somewhere else, but I'd end up at Bachelors III. We had decent food, but it wasn't a real sit down and eat type of joint. We went to drink, and basically just hang out and visit with the people who came in.

* * *

Then, on the night of June 3, 1969, I attended the New York football writers' banquet to receive the George Halas Award as the game's most courageous player. I don't know how they picked the most courageous award since there were a whole lot of us around the league playing through injuries. That said, it remains one of my most cherished trophies. Mr. Halas carried a lot of respect and his name was spoken with reverence, so I was humbled to receive any award with his endorsement.

I was there with one of the original five Jets owners and president, Phil Iselin. He got the message that somebody wanted to see both of us backstage, so we went and met an NFL security agent. He was talking to us, saying the NFL is demanding that I divest my interests in Bachelors III within forty-eight hours or I would be suspended from professional football due to the "unsavory people" who frequented it.

I looked at him and just said, "This is ridiculous. What are you, crazy?"

The next day, the NFL commissioner called and asked if my representative Jimmy Walsh and I could meet with him. We headed to Commissioner Rozelle's apartment on Madison Avenue. This was after we had to shake the media that waited outside my apartment building. A car took us to the New York Jets office on 57th Street where we picked up Mr. Iselin, but we snuck out a side door and into another car that took us to Rozelle's building unnoticed.

Before we started to discuss my situation, the commissioner pulled out a photo of me in my Jets uniform and asked if I could autograph it for his daughter, Anne Marie, because she was a fan of mine. That was the highlight of the meeting. I still disagreed with Commisioner Rozelle and repeated to him that I had done nothing wrong. He went on about how public faith in the game was essential. I agreed with him in that regard, but insisted that had nothing to do with me and my involvement in Bachelors III.

I explained I had no control over who came in. Thousands of customers came through Bachelors and I had no idea who almost all of them were. Any nightclub in New York would have "unsavory types" according to the NFL's definition.

This felt personal. I could see their point, but the way they handled it was lousy. In 1963, when I still was at

Alabama, the NFL had a real betting scandal on its hands. Paul Hornung and Alex Karras were suspended after they admitted to placing wagers on games and associating with gamblers or "known hoodlums," according to stories at that time. Hornung, a running back with the Green Bay Packers, was one of the NFL's most celebrated players, while Karras, a defensive lineman with the Detroit Lions, was an annual Pro Bowl selection. After their one-year suspension, Rozelle reinstated Hornung and Karras in 1964.

Some people think that situation may have contributed to the NFL's overreaction with Bachelors III, but I believe a lot of it had to do with the AFL beating the NFL in the Super Bowl. This was a personal affront on my character. I had never ever bet on any game. The NFL never accused me of that, just "associations with undesirables."

Rozelle said that while he didn't think I had done anything illegal, he felt I violated the provision in my contract that allowed him to suspend me if I was mingling with "gamblers and other notorious characters." I may have been saying "Hey, nice to see ya," but it wasn't like I was giving them our game plan. But Rozelle stuck to the deadline: sell my interest in Bachelors III within two days or he would suspend me from the NFL.

That was the first time in my life I realized on a grand stage that being right isn't always what matters. The demand was a real surprise and I felt that it was unfair, but also that I was being targeted for some other reason. Take a peek into some of the backgrounds of early football team owners and you'll run into what NFL security director Jack Danahy considered unsavory characters. But, for some reason, even though I was never accused of betting, I was going to have to lose my business with my friends, immediately.

Initially, I refused to sell my interest. At that time, the AFL and the NFL had agreed to merge. That's why the NFL representative was there breathing down hard on me. The NFL had a more historic reputation and a number of rules that just crossed the line, in my opinion, and went far beyond the game itself. Maybe my basic problem was that I never read any of the small print on my contract. Technically, I had never even signed an NFL contract, only two AFL contracts. I knew I was innocent of any wrongdoing, and that got me upset. It's like the one or two times in your life when you walk into the principal's office and you're innocent of the crime—you can go in with a little strut and you aren't afraid.

Among the things that bother me most in this world is hypocrisy, and the commissioner's demand of me was dripping in it. Here was a man who was willing to do business with Howard Hughes—who owned a bunch of Vegas casinos—and who had as owners of his teams men like Philip H. Iselin, who was also the president of Monmouth Park. I have always said I had no problem with the league doing a deal with Howard Hughes, and I was just fine with Mr. Iselin being president of a race track. But why would they have a problem with me running a business that had nothing to do with my work as quarterback just because people who liked to gamble happened to frequent my place?

From a financial point of view, Mike, Jimmy, and others advised me to sell. I stood to lose millions from my Jets contract and all sorts of endorsements if I quit playing football. I knew they were right, that selling was the smart solution. But I also knew it was wrong and against everything I believed in and stood for. I was hurt and angry.

We decided to hold the press conference the following morning at Bachelors III—where else? We arrived at the club around ten a.m., and the place was packed. I sat down at a table between Frank Gifford and Kyle Rote, two great football Hall of Famers who also became famous for commentating. Howard Cosell, who first practiced law in Manhattan before becoming a sportscaster, was at one end of the table. There were more than a dozen microphones set up in front of me. I told the crowd that I wasn't divesting my interest in Bachelors III, and that I was retiring from professional football. I said I had never bet on the sport, which was the only thing the commissioner should be concerned about. Selling would send the wrong message and I was taking a stand. I felt like I'd been slapped by that nun again, so I was going to throw my books out the window.

Before I was done, tears were running down my face. They were tears of anger from the accusations and sadness over the loss of football, which had been my life since childhood. It felt like the end, and it hit me right then as I said it out loud. A number of my teammates, including Jim Hudson, George Sauer, and Pete Lammons—three of our Texans—told reporters if I didn't play in the upcoming 1969 season, they wouldn't play, either. I appreciated their support but didn't want them to quit on my account. My mother, father, and brothers also called, and nobody seemed upset with my decision. Besides, Mom was worried about my injured knees, anyway. They wanted me to do what I felt was right. I went back to Bachelors III that night, not so much to celebrate but to relax, and there was a line to get in. At least business was still good. And all the publicity led to multiple inquiries from folks across the country wanting to open other Bachelors III establishments. It sure looked like a great investment.

But it also wasn't professional football.

Once I made that decision, had the press conference, and came to terms with what a life outside football really meant, I began to feel incredibly alone. Then I also started getting stir-crazy. My life was out of balance. This was the first time since childhood that I wasn't participating in a physical activity, a sport, that I loved. There had been a serious lack of preparation going into making the decision, and while I still felt it was the right one, I had no plan for the future. I'd take a football and go over to Central Park and find some guys to throw to and catch with. I'd even bring some pals from Bachelors III like "Stevie Ice Cream" or "Larry Lawyer" or "Petey the Greek," or "Captain Video." We'd play a little touch football. I even played softball in the Broadway show league. I was on the *Promises, Promises* team. I *needed* to be doing something physical. But also had no idea what to do with myself.

The media jumped on the story. *Life* magazine called Bachelors III a "hoodlum-haunted" place. *Newsweek* and *Sports Illustrated* did stories, too. *Sports Illustrated* reported about craps games that supposedly took place in my Manhattan apartment in January and February of 1969. I wasn't even in New York for those months. Following the Super Bowl, I was actually visiting wounded soldiers in army hospitals in Okinawa and Guam, Hawaii, and the Philippines, and relaxing at my winter home in Miami. My mother read one of the stories and called me up crying. Slaughtering the name, she asked me to stop hanging out with the "Costa Reesa guys." I understood that she was trying to say Cosa Nostra.

As this was going on, Jimmy said, "Never pick a fight with a guy who buys ink by the barrel."

My response: "Why didn't you tell me that a few years ago!" It brought me back to Mrs. Werblin, who understood this whole process and had explained it to me over that dinner so long ago: This was show business. It was entertainment and it sold magazines.

Then rumors started to get even wilder. Some people said it was all a publicity stunt for Bachelors III, others felt my ego was getting in the way of doing the sensible thing and just selling my stake.

But I always had a mixed relationship with the media. It was during my rookie year at training camp when a crew of writers sat in the bleachers watching practice. The pool was full of reporters from every city that had an AFL team. They had been visiting all the training camps prior to the season. Frank Ramos, the Jets media director, approached me after practice and said it was my turn to talk to the writers. I walked over, and they clearly saw this spoiled kid with a big contract as a fresh piece of prime meat that they were going to enjoy carving into.

One reporter held up his pencil as if he was going to ask an important question, his notepad in his other hand. I looked at him, assuming this was how it went, and he asked, "I understand you went to the University of Alabama. What did you major in there, basket weaving?"

I gave that some thought—about a split second's worth—and then answered, "Yeah, basket weaving was pretty tough, though, so I dropped it and took up journalism."

Some of these guys laughed, reminding me of the older pool hall sharks hanging around the tables when I played. You learned pretty quick how to read a person, and how to, respectfully, with as much edge as they gave it, give it back. I thought that was an apropos comment. The smart-aleck scribe got what he deserved.

Everyone, though, wanted to find a solution that would let me rejoin my teammates. Meanwhile, the Jets opened training camp on July 13, but I didn't report—contrary to stories that were being published by the sports media.

During that time, I'd also spend a lot of time at Central Park by myself. I'd walk into the park off the south corner of 79th and Fifth, stroll around, and end up sitting on the high mound of Dog Hill. It was one of my favorite spots in the city to be alone. Up there, you can see Fifth Avenue and the people running their pups, lost in their own worlds. Everywhere I looked I saw people so full of life, and here I was sitting on my butt doing nothing. None of these folks cared even a *little* bit about what I did. This fight, the retirement, was only huge to me. The world was going on regardless.

I sat there thinking about my teammates in training camp. I wanted to get back to life, get back to the football that I missed severely.

So I called Jimmy, who called the Jets and gave them a heads-up. Respectfully, they had to be contacted first. Then Jimmy began the process of selling my percentage in Bachelors III in New York but retained the right to invest—with Ray and Bobby as my partners—in other Bachelors III bars in other cities. We opened clubs in Boston, Fort Lauderdale, Tuscaloosa, and Birmingham.

I was involved in restaurants for about another ten years

and I must have fit the character somewhat as years later, my movie agent, Mike Greenfield, came to me about a television show set in a bar and suggested I was perfect for the character who owned the establishment. That character's name was Sam Malone and the series was *Cheers*. But watching that show, I wouldn't have had a chance of getting the role going against Ted Danson. They obviously chose the right guy. He was sensational. I was also given the script for *M*A*S*H*. I don't know if I even read the whole thing. I was ignorant about the whole process of going out for parts. I had no concept of what was good or not, zero ability to visualize how it might turn out. There was no way I could have competed against Alan Alda at his level. And, hey, I got to enjoy both from my living room.

One job I did know I was right for, though, was being the quarterback for the New York Jets. So with all the parts in place, we met with Commissioner Rozelle on a Friday. That Sunday evening, I reported to Jets camp at Hofstra University on Long Island, New York.

My retirement had lasted about a month, but it got to feeling so long that I couldn't wait to get out to camp. Life isn't always fair, but we need to learn to deal with it. And, come on, we're talking about professional football, a game, after all. Nobody cared but me, so I learned a lesson about reality right then. I also got schooled in how an employer's perception works—the facts didn't matter as much as the optics. I could have, I think, gone to court and won, but that would have dragged it all out.

I just wanted to play again.

CHAPTER TWELVE

The clouds have mostly passed over my house. I wonder if I'll be able to get my workout in the pool later tonight or if another storm will blow in.

I look at my notes on the counter. I love writing notes. Maybe it has something to do with keeping my brain firing and organized. I check as best I can for traces of degeneration, and so far, I've been lucky. Degeneration or not, though, memories and time can sure get jumbled when you watch an event that had a major impact on your life but has been documented so thoroughly.

I glance around at the family pictures pinned on the wall in my kitchen, just like plays on the chalkboards during those regular team and position meetings. Man, that regular schedule was a big part of my life. A typical day would start with a team meeting at high noon. I had to leave the house at eleven and change if we were at Shea Stadium. If I had to go to Long Island, I had to leave a little earlier. Or, if the offensive coordinator wanted to talk to me, then I usually got there maybe half an hour earlier, otherwise I'd have to wait until after practice at four.

Practice might not start on the field until two or two-thirty. There was a general meeting to start with, when the head coach talked to both the offense and the defense. Then we broke up and went into our position meetings: the o-linemen, the running backs, the receivers, and the quarterbacks. The defensive team would break up with the linebackers working with both the defensive linemen and the defensive backs. The special teams meetings would cover the entire kicking game. We'd be on the field maybe two hours. Practices never had full contact, since players were usually beat up from the week before, and rosters were limited to around forty players on a team. Today's game-day roster is fifty-three.

Afterward, I'd drive back to the city and do my home-work and then go out. Almost every night. Starting a family wasn't even a thought back then. I just wasn't ready for that type of game. With the women I'd meet during my Jets days, I was up-front with them that I wasn't looking for a long-term relationship. I didn't want to hurt anybody, so I made that as clear as I could. I didn't date any ladies exclusively. In fact, I didn't live with a woman until 1984, when I was forty-one. And I ended up marrying her.

In New York, I enjoyed the dating freedom, and I had a good balance. I needed the open space on the football field to run around in and breathe clean air deeply, and then I could also start almost every night exiting my East Side apartment and begin hitting some of my favorite night spots, including PJ Clarke's for a late snack, the Pussycat, Dudes 'n Dolls, Tittle Tattle, the Open End, the Gobbler's Knob, Playboy Club, and the Golden 20s. Maybe even the Copacabana. As I mentioned, Weeb had such late practice starts that I could easily fit in all my activities. A little film study for upcoming games, a practice for maybe a total of four hours, some drinks, then a good meal with friends and plenty of good talk, and then a few more drinks, and then hopefully company into the early morning, maybe play the hi-fi as we got cozy. If I got it all wrapped up by three in the morning, there was still time to grab my seven hours of sleep. I was a man who appreciated my routine.

I was in my early twenties when this fame hit, living in one of the sexiest cities in the world. So it felt natural to just turn toward it and not shy away. I enjoyed the company of ladies and, man, were there a lot of places servicing the singles crowd.

This was the late 1960s and 1970s—the era of sexual revolution, and a decade before AIDS hit the scene and changed everything with regard to safety and partners. There was a freedom allowed, and the people I came into contact with after a certain hour were determined not to waste it. Like I said, I was honest, so there were no illusions about long-term relationships.

I wanted to enjoy life, and the attention I received was just a part of living in New York, where newspapers fill the celebrity gossip cycle. I unwittingly obliged by being at a lot of the watering holes where they photographed people around town, so there was a reputation created that wasn't expected for an athlete at the time.

The AFL's sensibility about football being entertainment was not sugarcoated. The *Sports Illustrated* cover that got me my nickname not only had me standing on Broadway, but it said FOOTBALL GOES SHOW BIZ beside me. The AFL needed New York City. The team owner, Mr. Werblin, had always stated that stars sell tickets, and I was the physical manifestation of that mantra. I sure wasn't complaining though, and I did okay in that role.

Partly due to the fame around my playing for the Jets, the "Broadway Joe" nickname, and my friendship with Mr. Werblin, there were frequent get-togethers with celebrity actors and actresses. I'd be invited to Mr. Werblin's apartment and Johnny Carson might stroll in. One time he had a couple of drinks—we all had more than a couple of drinks, actually—and Johnny gets this attitude, all huffing and puffing, and he goes up to Sauer and starts talking trash to him. Everybody got a little quiet, wondering what was going on, as Johnny says that football players think they're so tough and slaps George across the face.

Ralph Baker, a six-four linebacker and a real gentleman, pulled Johnny away. Well, Johnny got lucky and slapped the right player because Sauer, a sweetheart of a guy, gave no reaction. If he had hit another Texan named Jim Hudson, Johnny's career might have ended right then. I'm glad it didn't, because I always enjoyed watching Johnny and his *Tonight Show*. I think the prospect of being lifted and thrown across the room sobered Johnny up, and he stopped his shenanigans.

I actually had that story wrong for forty-odd years, and it wasn't until Baker corrected me at a Jets reunion and pointed out that Sauer, and not him, was the one who got the slap that I realized the mix-up. Strange how the mind works but memory fades. I head into the living room with my iPad and sit down. After double checking to make sure the sound is still off, I settle down and press play.

THIRD QUARTER

CHAPTER THIRTEEN

Curley starts the second half with the opening kickoff. He knew the Colts' return man, Preston Pearson, led the NFL in kick-return yardage and saw him on the right side, so he kicked high and left, two yards deep into the end zone. Timmy Brown brought it out until our kick team stopped him at the 24-yard line. Not enough credit is given to the coverage team on kickoffs. I want to say right now that they did a great job. Not only did Curley keep the ball away from Preston, we'd stopped the Colts from running a big return twice at this point.

The score is 7–0, advantage Jets. But there was absolutely nobody on our sideline who felt comfortable with that lead. Again, our opponents were the Baltimore Colts—one of the best professional football teams ever assembled up to that point in history. Being up by a touchdown, with a whole half left to play? It was nice, but there was a lot of game left.

I have no recollection of where I was standing during the kick, but I do remember the lights coming on as the afternoon sun had transformed into an evening twilight. On the broadcast, you can see the white lights reflecting off our helmets, making it impossible to focus on anything but the action on the field. And right away that's just what there is. On the first play of the second half, Tom Matte took a handoff up the middle and after fighting for about seven yards, defensive end Verlon Biggs laid the wood on Matte, knocking the ball loose, and our linebacker Ralph Baker recovered the fumble. Our defense created a great opportunity with that turnover in the Colts' backyard.

I knew that getting points even from the Colts' 33-yard line was going to be a challenge. Getting into the huddle, I was expecting that Baltimore wasn't going to make any defensive changes. After all, we only have seven points on the board—it's not as if we're beating their defense up. Until they take away that simple handoff to the outside, we're gonna keep runnin' it. Take what they give you.

First-and-10. I handed off to Boozer, who bolted for eight yards, right behind the blockers who'd been affording an effective running game. It's through that same gap on our offensive left side that we'd been taking advantage of since the first quarter. Now it was Snell's turn. Second down and only two yards to go. He heads right up the middle for a four-yard gain and another Jets first down.

Looking at the plays, I notice the same fundamentals dealing with my footwork that were taught to me by Coach Bruno back in high school. I wasn't going to be the first-string quarterback my junior year, but Coach Bruno knew that I could be a player with some help, so that summer before my junior year he asked me to come over to his house to help clean up the yard. Linwood and I found our way over to Coach Bruno's place and started to work. And when we got close to finishing, he took me aside and explained what we were going to start doing, football-wise. He began showing me footwork right then and there.

I'm using all of that now, with a seven-point lead, and driving in the Colts' red zone, where we've gotta get at least three points. That means we're not going to be overly risky. I don't know if our kicker, Jim Turner, went through a game missing two or three field goals. He might have, but I don't recall it. He was a good field-goal kicker, real reliable. But that position can be nerve-wracking.

In fact, having never been a kicker, I just can't imagine the emotional pressure. Very often a game hinges on their success or failure. So many things can go wrong. The center has to deliver the ball accurately. The holder has to catch it and place it properly. The blocking has to hold. The kicker's plant foot can't slip. Then he has to hit it straight. Any one of those six things go wrong, and what seems like an easy kick can go bad. Then you factor in Mother Nature with winds and rain. But kickers are a different breed of football player. They are unique, and I don't at all mean that in a derogatory sense. Bottom line: Kicking extra points or field goals isn't a cinch.

I remember feeling good, though, knowing that if we didn't manage to cross the goal line, we'd still be able to add to our margin.

Still, being so deep in an opponent's territory has its challenges. Defensively, there's an advantage because they have less field to cover, which means they can crowd players up toward the line to stop the run. To make matters even more complicated, on that first down I see now that they did give us a little bit of a different look. We were strong side left, and they matched our strong side with a linebacker over the tight end.

Watching it now, I wonder why I didn't run Eighteen-straight. Oh wait, I know why—Bubba Smith was over there up against Dave Herman, our smallest offensive line-man, and asking him to block Bubba one-on-one felt like asking too much. Dave had heart, but it was somewhat of a physical mismatch—we were all a mismatch compared to Bubba. That's why we ran it the other way. Having to do it again, I wouldn't have called that formation strong left. We became locked in to running left.

I ran Boozer. After a two-yard gain, the broadcast flashes to the sideline and there he is. Johnny U warming up! Until now, I had no idea that was happening so early on.

On second down I decided to throw a pass with all five receivers going downfield. While dropping back, I saw Snell wide open on a wide swing route. I didn't set up to throw because I didn't need to—I could get the ball out of there without planting my feet. I delivered and he got us a first down.

On the next series, I notice they aren't in the same short-yardage defense that they normally played. In the huddle, I called a "check with me" and when we got to the line of scrimmage I saw the split between the defensive tackles and called the run audible: "Eleven!" This sent Snell straight ahead between our left guard and our center.

It was first-and-10. Do we throw? Turns out not. Instead, I handed the ball off to Boozer, who immediately got swarmed by a partially blocked Rick Volk. Boozer managed to shake Volk loose but eventually is stopped for a five-yard loss. The guys in blue shirts were in pretty good pursuit.

Then I watch the next play and realize that I got sacked not once, but twice in the game. Until that moment, I swear I only thought I got tackled with the ball once. On second-and-15, Bubba comes barreling around the corner and I just didn't see it coming until it was too late. He wrapped me up like a rag doll, taking me to the ground.

But Dave, our right tackle with the heart of a pit bull, had a tough assignment against Bubba. Before the season, Weeb had the foresight to know that he might have issues with his two rookie offensive linemen on our right side, so he had talked former Houston Oiler offensive lineman Bob Talamini out of retirement. If we had a problem at right offensive tackle, Coach Ewbank could plug Bob in at left guard and move Dave to the right offensive tackle position. And he did just that against Oakland. Dave played right tackle for the first time in his professional life against the Raiders—in that brutal AFL Championship Game that got us here.

The Raiders' left defensive end, Ike Lassiter, was a beast who weighed three hundred pounds. I remember seeing Dave in the locker room after that game and being so impressed. He did such a great job. He played out of position in two of the most important games of our lives against two of the best defensive ends in the sport of football. As a novice, he was lining up against two All-Pros, each fifty pounds heavier, and we ended up winning both competitions.

Deciding what to run on third-and-24 is never easy, especially if you're in field goal range. You don't want to make a major mistake and lose out on field goal position. And this next play, one I remember well, proved why it's difficult.

While dropping back to pass, I saw Lammons curling up underneath defensive back Jerry Logan. Protection was good, so I was able to set up. I put as much heat on the ball as possible to Pete's outside because Logan was closing fast from the inside. With that much velocity, passes can be difficult to catch. Logan reached out, touched it, but it was too hot and it burned through his hands. So it goes.

Jim Turner came on. He put it through the uprights and now we were up 10–0. Sure felt better than 7–0, but again, with this much time left in the game, things are far from over. In fact, ever since the infamous "Heidi" game in November of 1968, we didn't dare consider the game being finished until the final whistle blew.

We were leading in that game, and like all Oakland contests, it was brutal, just a bloody battle of wills, in which everybody was giving and taking heavy and, often, late hits. Maybe an extra elbow into the jock strap areas or a twist of the face mask, or taking a little longer to get back up off me. Things became so chippy that, in the third quarter, Jim Hudson got booted from the game after fighting with the ref over a face mask penalty. Maybe that's why Frank Ramos used to just refer to those games as "wars."

During the final minute, as we kicked off to the Raiders, the television broadcast abruptly switched to the sweet family movie *Heidi*, about a sweet young girl in the Alps that...well, let's just say it was the exact opposite atmosphere of what was happening in our game. With one minute remaining, most people watching on TV assumed we had won, but Oakland scored two touchdowns in under sixty seconds, and handed us an L that stung in the way only an Oakland loss back then could.

After that game, former Cleveland Browns linebacker Walt Michaels, now our defensive coordinator, wanted to talk to the game officials. They wouldn't acknowledge his insistent knocking on their locker room door, so he put a good shoulder into it a couple times and got it open. He gave them a piece of his mind about the calls and Hudson's ejection.

I had been in rivalry games before and knew how raw emotions could get, but the Oakland Raiders took that to another level. And it's clear to me that losing the way we did was of great service, a real coachable moment as they say, that we carried with us the rest of the season and into that next series as our defense forced the Colts to go three and out. Once again, they stopped the Colts from coming close to a score.

When we get the ball back at our own 32-yard line, I'm feeling inspired by our D and good physically, even though our offensive line is probably tired as hell. Matt Snell should be the most exhausted player on our team. He's been blocking, running the ball more than anyone else, catching passes, as well as running downfield covering kickoffs and punts. Unheard of today.

I see he's finally taking a break.

On first down, I hit Mathis on a medium flare route for a good gain. I felt good about the pass protection and decided to throw again. George ran that square in-route, the same one he ran earlier in the game. He might have brought it in a bit further, but it's the little "out and in" move that he was so good at. Man, was he great at it.

Fourteen yards later we had another first-and-10. Remember the two I overthrew Maynard on in the first half? Because of those tries, you can bet that the Colts defense was rotating to take away the deep threat from Maynard. He was a lightning strike to every defense we played against. Teams don't want to give up the big play, the long gainer. Considering he hadn't practiced all week, I'm still surprised by how often we threw to him. You know, even incompletions can have positive effects in the long term. So I dropped back, the protection was perfect, and I see Don a step ahead of his coverage man. I did what I always did when I saw Don open—I threw to him! The ball ended up a few feet outside his grasp.

Now NBC cuts to a wide shot of the Dodge Charger that *Sport* magazine gave away as a bonus to the game's MVP. It wasn't the exact car they're showing, the reddish orange one. How do I know? Because I won the thing and gave it to my mother. She'd never driven a car before and can you believe it? A Dodge Charger as your first ride at her age? The engine had some horsepower, man. I let her drive me exactly one time and that was enough for me. After that, I always drove. The Oakland Raiders were a scary squad to go up against, but they had nothing on sitting shotgun while my mom attempted to handle a muscle car down an avenue in Beaver Falls. But, heck, she used that thing for years.

When they get back to the action, I see it's second-and-10 and I called a quick draw play to Boozer, before hitting our tight end Pete Lammons for eleven yards over the middle and another first down. We were moving the ball nicely now. We were consistently completing passes. Or almost completing. At the line of scrimmage on the next play, I notice how deep the defender is playing over Don and I audible to a quick out, which is knocked out of Don's hands after a vicious tackle by Bobby Boyd.

That gives us second-and-10. Once again, thank you offensive line, protection has been good, so we go to the passing game and hit Matt Snell for a fourteen-yard gainer right up the middle.

Now we're on the Colts' 24-yard line and Mathis gets a carry up the middle, before I take another shot at Maynard on second down. And there Maynard goes. I put it where only he could get it, which in this case was just outside the end zone. Maynard extended fully to reel it in. Had the end zone been about two yards longer, that grab would have gone down in history.

On that throw you can see my hand hit a defender's helmet and even all these decades later, I can remember how much my damn right thumb hurt. This wasn't the first time that I had injured that thumb, either. It had bothered me for the last month of the season. I had to get off the field. I didn't let anybody touch it, not even the trainers. The pain was acute and I tried to shake it off. Meanwhile, my backup and boyhood hero, the fifteen-year vet, Babe Parilli, was rushed out there without any chance to warm up his throwing arm and ended up missing Sauer on a quick in.

Watching this now, I'm wondering if we should have called a time-out, just so we didn't rush Parilli in there cold, give him a chance to warm up. But there is no way I would have come off the field if I had been sure that I would have been able to handle the ball on the next play.

Before getting to the next play, my daughter Jessica comes in with a parade of barking dogs and tells me about a chiropractor she found for me. I pause the video.

"He says his dad was your original center when you got on the Jets."

* * *

John Matlock was that center. My daughter says she made me an appointment and gives me the card with the date and time on it. I give her a hug and a kiss on the cheek and think about how lucky I am to have my daughters in my life, and know that they are relatively happy and safe. They know how proactive I am about my health.

That winter of '69, I'd done some work with the USO, which was important to me considering I was never healthy enough myself to be in the service. Just to be sure, though, in 1965, the military had me do three physicals before the surgeon general issued a report to Congress detailing why Joe Namath, who was playing professional football at the time, was 4-F, physically incapable of going to battle. My first physical was at White Hall in New York City with hundreds of other recruits, and the other two were with privately assigned doctors to make sure my knee was really as messed up as purported. Blowing my knee out certainly negatively affected me as a football player, but it might also have saved my life.

After our Jets won the Super Bowl, I did a USO tour with sports announcer Charlie Jones, Giants offensive tackle Steve Allen, Oakland Raiders center Jim Otto, and Green Bay Packers tight end Marv Fleming. That was an unforgettable experience and a special glimpse into the human condition, seeing these great big smiles of joy coming from soldiers who were in such pain. Some were a lot younger than I was, they looked like kids, and that truth created complex feelings. I have a bum knee? I'm seeing kids without legs.

We went into wards where they hadn't removed the deceased yet, still in beds with sheets over their heads. The burn wards were particularly hard, the injuries looked so painful…it's hard to put into words. There were guys missing limbs and others in traction with casts up to their necks, heads completely wrapped. The last guy we saw was a quadruple amputee in Tripler hospital in Honolulu, Hawaii, and he had a machine on the side of his bed to help with his insides while he was talking to us.

But those warriors, boy, they just wanted to talk to me about the game. They'd smile and laugh and I really felt thankful for the opportunity to be able to share those powerful moments with them.

* * *

I've become enlightened on the importance of connecting with people and remember a time when I had to break the biggest connection of my professional career. By 1977, I had been with the Jets for a dozen years. I wanted to still play but didn't feel that I was the best fit for the team anymore. After a losing season, I was having dinner with the Jets' principal owners, Mr. and Mrs. Hess. We were talking about our future and there was a rumor I was leaving for the Rams. My Jets contract was up and the Hesses wanted me to stay and help with the team as a mentor.

They were rebuilding, but I wanted to play still and didn't feel that I belonged there. I felt I would be more of a distraction than a help. They needed to start another quarterback. I knew my time was short as a player, and I wanted to be on a contender. So I left New York for Los Angeles and spent my last season with the Rams. The LA team was being led by a head coach that I had known for years—Chuck Knox.

He had previously been an offensive line coach with the Jets and encouraged the organization to draft me in 1965.

On May 12, 1977, I signed with the Rams.

I was excited to move to LA, too. I met the owner, Carroll Rosenbloom, at his mansion in Bel Air. The area was beautiful. The butler let me in and the house service was all buttoned up and highfalutin' as they began presenting us with the food. The meal looked amazing, and as I started to dig in, I reached for the salt shaker.

"Joseph, put that down!"

Mr. Rosenbloom was in his sixties, and I looked at him with respect. He was the man. And he had said it rather loud.

"I just got out of the hospital for high blood pressure. I had a coronary condition that nearly killed me. Salt was a main culprit."

Man, I loved salt—I used to put it on watermelon, on so many things. As a kid, I carried a salt shaker on me! After that, I stopped using salt at home and in restaurants.

That may have been the best part of my move to the Rams. It was certainly my healthiest.

Health, indeed, was a bit of an issue when I got to California. There was the air quality that took some getting used to. At training camp it burned my throat and eyes and obscured the scenery for my first week. Then the smog cleared one day, and I looked over surprised to see mountains around us. But I also had problems that could not be blamed on pollution. During games, when the Rams came screaming out of the dressing room in the Coliseum, they had a tradition of running the length of the field along the sideline and then breaking across the field into rows to do calisthenics. It was all I could do to keep up. My left leg wouldn't straighten out after that hamstring injury, and I was scared I was going to fall over just trying to keep pace. I was thirty-four and, considering my five knee surgeries, beginning to feel like a senior veteran.

The Rams were a good team and on their way to the playoffs. At that age, transitioning playbooks also proved difficult. Starting with how they numbered the gaps in the offensive line. Since Pop Warner, from the center over was even numbers right, odd numbers left. But Chuck Knox's system was different. Odd numbers were right and even left. You could catch on, but that extra bit of thinking was problematic. Chuck also insisted on sending in the first-down and third-down plays, instead of letting me call the shots like I had done since forever.

To make matters worse, that was also the first time a coach tried to change my passing motion. The guy in charge of the quarterbacks didn't like it when we patted the ball before we threw, which for me proved essential. In preparation for almost every pass, that pre-throw pat would help coil my left side under my chin so I could get good velocity on the ball. Not patting changed my upper shoulder coil. Out of respect, I did what the coach asked, but I lost that coil and the extra velocity it created. Being in my thirteenth year of professional football and using the same passing motion since my childhood, in hindsight, I was wrong to try to change it.

The last game I played in was against the Bears up in Chicago. It was a Monday night contest, on the shores of Lake Michigan. The Bears had a pair of safeties on the team, Gary Fencik and Doug Plank, one of whom caught my last pass in professional football. I distinctly remember because it was a good hit on me. I didn't even get to see the interception because I took a helmet in the chest just as I released the pass. Then the back of my head bounced off the ground. I was told about it after I was helped up. We came off the field, and when we got possession back, Coach Knox put Pat Haden in. He started for the rest of the season and played well.

On a cool night in the Los Angeles Memorial Coliseum on December 26, 1977, our Rams played the Minnesota Vikings for the divisional title. The stadium was a sloppy mess from an earlier rainfall. It was just a pile of mud between the hash marks. Later, it was referred to as the Mud Bowl, and the Vikings won, 14–7.

There was one moment in that game, man. Must have been late third or early fourth quarter, when we were behind. I was standing near Coach Knox and he turned and glanced in my direction. We made eye contact and he gave me a look, the sort that was subtly asking if I had something left in the tank for one more comeback. I didn't give him anything back, though. We just looked into each other's eyes, a few seconds went by, and he glanced back out to the field.

I've often thought about that moment.

I really feel like I let him down.

In retrospect, that was the first time I dug deep only to discover that I didn't have the confidence to compete.

The day before the game was the only time I'd ever spent Christmas alone. And, boy, did I ever feel alone. At around ten at night, I decided to go for a stroll, so I walked out of my rental duplex in Belmont Shores and headed south.

The back door was on the beach and I headed toward the water. Normally, I might have carried a drink with me, but for some reason, I didn't that night. I just walked, looking around, thinking about what was happening and how everything seemed so big and empty. I didn't see a single person. I'm walking and thinking, What am I doing?

I was all by myself, and I glanced down at my flip-flops and the sand around my feet. I headed toward the jetty and climbed up on the rocks and found a place to sit. I just looked around, feeling the loneliness. I was thinking about all the grains of sand and the vastness above in the black sky full of stars, and it hit me, how insignificant I was in the universe.

What was next for me? I knew I wasn't going to play pro ball anymore after this season. I was thrilled to be on the Rams, and the coaches, players, and trainers were terrific guys. I can't recall a bum on the team. The realization that I was so small and trivial in the makeup of things helped put everything in perspective.

On Dog Hill I had been lonely and missed football and my teammates. But this, this was a deeper, more expansive furtherance of those feelings. I had to continue and be a part of something. Looking back, I'm thankful for that moment, for being alone and how that helped me connect with the greater energy out there.

CHAPTER FOURTEEN

I turn back to the screen, press play, and see we're on the Colts' 23-yard line. After Babe's pass, it's fourth down. No other option here but to kick the field goal. Our kicker, Jim Turner, another one of our backup quarterbacks as well as a wide receiver, trotted on and took care of business, giving us Jets a 13–0 lead.

Curley came on and kicked the ball through the end zone. This may seem casual or insignificant, but a touchback is huge, as it eliminates the Colts from getting a big gainer or a fast score. As I'm on the phone with offensive coordinator, Clive Rush, my hand was already feeling better. The Colts fans, though—they finally had a reason to cheer and I could feel the ground rumble. It was a strong moment. It was Johnny U coming in to save the day! Watching this broadcast is the first time I realize that Unitas played this early. For all these years, I thought he didn't get into the game until the fourth quarter, when we were up by more than thirteen.

Regardless of Lou Michaels's aggressive confidence in

Johnny, I knew Unitas still wasn't himself. He had a reputation for coming in late and clinching games, but he was injured and had been most of the year. Really, he wasn't even close to himself and couldn't throw with his usual velocity. That said, there was always concern from the other teams when Johnny came out. He always charged up his squad, and according to tradition, his team was about to make a comeback.

My favorite memory of Johnny isn't even from one of the battles we had on the field, though. Those were fun, sure. But the memory I cherish the most is sitting next to him on a barstool at a golf tournament in Nevada in the 1970s. He and I ended up being the last two in the establishment late one night. Sitting there at the bar, just talking, was unforgettable for me. Man, he was the boss. He was the senior guy and I sat there and listened to him with all the respect in the world. We were both from western Pennsylvania and I had watched him for so long, all the way back to when I was a teenager struggling just to make the team..

Full disclosure here: The only reason I had gotten the QB job on our ninth-grade team was because our starter—a guy bigger, faster, stronger, and mentally more mature than me—had broken his hand.

Going into tenth grade, I wasn't even invited to the early football training camp. It was put on in the summer and supported by the Beaver Falls booster club.

I was small. So small, in fact, that I had prayed to St. Jude to get taller, but he hadn't answered yet. It shouldn't have been any surprise that I wasn't invited to that preseason camp. But it was the first time I had never made the team. I was hurt. I was sad. Most of my friends went off to it and I was left alone. My buddy Ray was a senior, and he was one of us, the three football players who didn't get invited.

"Yeah...I'm just gonna quit," he said.

I'd never thought of that, but it was an option, wasn't it? It would end the hurt.

"When they get back, let's go up and quit."

They returned, and Ray and I were waiting for Coach Ross outside the locker room before first practice. Coach comes out and Ray says, "Coach, I'm going to quit."

"Well, you're a senior and you know what you want to do. Best of luck to you."

Then he looked at me. "Coach, I'm going to quit, too." I thought I needed to give him a reason. "I'm going to focus on basketball and baseball."

Coach gave me a thoughtful look.

"Well, Joe...I don't know. I think you should stay. I think you can be a player."

That was all I needed. I didn't want to quit, but I was hurt. I didn't have a uniform. I didn't have a locker. I wasn't part of the team.

But I did get a uniform and wore it to haul out the tackling dummies all season long. We were the practice squad that went against the better team, but I'd take every opportunity to show the coaches that I could play.

By the end of that season St. Jude answered my prayers, and by my junior year I had shot up a full head in height.

That was Coach Ross's last season before he was promoted to athletic director of Beaver Falls High School. His first move, and it was a great one, was hiring Coach Bruno from nearby Monaca High School. Coach Bruno was my first great coach and mentor, so much so that I asked him to introduce me for my induction into the Pro Football Hall of Fame.

Prior to the Super Bowl, the selection committee picks players, coaches, owners, general managers, commissioners, and administrators to induct. I was eligible after five years and was picked in the eighth year. The Hall of Fame is a tremendous honor considering the company you keep. I didn't earn my way into the Hall of Fame by myself—it was a team effort with my former coaches and teammates. So when I was told to pick somebody to introduce me, I started thinking about the three men who had the most impact on my football life: Coach Bruno, Coach Bryant, and Coach Ewbank. Coach Bryant had passed away at age seventy in 1983. I called Coach Ewbank.

"I've been asked to pick somebody to introduce me for my Hall of Fame induction. You were my pro coach so you are the first man I thought about. I also thought about my high school mentor, Coach Bruno who—"

Weeb cut me off. "Go ahead and get Larry!"

Weeb had been there for my growth as a professional. We had won a Super Bowl together. "Coach, I—"

"Joe! Shucks! I'm already in the Hall of Fame. Get Larry."

Coach Ewbank made it easy. He knew how important he had been to me, but he was also understanding of how critical Coach Bruno had been to me in my life.

I was excited to call Coach Bruno, and he, in his soft voice, said, "Oh, jeez, Joe. Of course. Thank you."

I was inducted with Roger "the Dodger" Staubach, and we sat next to each other in Canton, Ohio. I was a big fan of him from his days playing for the Naval Academy, and had learned to respect fellow inductee NFL commissioner Pete Rozelle after the Bachelors III situation. I knew OJ Simpson from some television work, and it was an honor meeting Frank Gatski, one of the earliest pro football players.

I was thrilled when Don Maynard got inducted into the Hall of Fame two years later. And it was such an honor when he asked me to introduce him. Don continues to inspire me. Just thinking about him makes me break out into a smile. Maynard was the first Jets teammate I met during my initial visit to the locker room at Shea Stadium. I'd be there for the next twelve years, but right then I was in awe.

That day, offensive line Coach Chuck Knox and Frank Ramos led me into the locker room with a group of sportswriters, and Don was at his locker. Equipment manager Bill Hampton took me over to meet Don, who had his back to me. After the introduction, Don took my shoulder and turned me away from the writers and said, "Son, I'm goin' to tell you something. All these people are patting you on the back and shaking your hand right now, but when they're finished with you, they may not even say good-bye. This is a cold-blooded business."

I never heard Maynard say a curse word or saw him touch a drink. As Don and I became closer, I had to ask him why he never drank or cursed. He said that he had promised his granddaddy that he would never swear or drink and kept his word. Talk about dedication. This was a man who believed in his own ability. Imagine getting cut from NFL teams, going to play in Canada, and then working your way onto a new team in a new league before finally getting into the Hall of Fame. Incredible.

As for Coach Bruno, I got to see him every time I went back to Beaver Falls. He coached our Tiger team for nineteen years. He was instrumental in getting me into Alabama and talked to Coach Bryant about me. I had assumed that Coach Bryant didn't know anything about me prior to me going to Alabama, but I learned that in my sophomore season when he called me "Babe" he was talking about Babe Parilli, who he coached at Kentucky and who was also from western Pennsylvania. Parilli's hometown, Rochester, was only four miles south of Beaver Falls and we both hailed from the Beaver Valley. When I was growing up, the Army and Navy store in Beaver Falls had a gold Hutch helmet signed by Babe, and I used to go look and marvel at the signature on it. And now Babe was the one who came in for me in the Super Bowl when I hurt my hand! His locker that year was next to mine, and I still marveled at how surreal it felt. Here I was putting on a Jets helmet with him. It was wonderful. Nice guy, but I only played gin with him one time. Learned my lesson quick.

I also didn't know Coach Bryant had coached the great George Blanda, who played pro football for an incredible twenty-six seasons. When George first arrived at the University of Kentucky, where Coach Bryant led the Wildcats at the time, George apparently only had one set of clothes and used a rope as his belt. George himself told me the story about Coach reaching into his own pocket and giving him money to get some clothes.

Thinking about how all the people in my life connect has always been a joy for me.

But fast-forward back to that empty bar in Nevada, me on the barstool next to Johnny, and I felt like that kid again—the one about to quit the football team. Heck, growing up, I was a Baltimore Colts fan. We even had a guy from Beaver Falls, Jim Mutscheller, who played tight end for them. And then there was the 1958 Championship Game between the

New York Giants and the Baltimore Colts, which, at one time, was called "The Greatest Game Ever Played."

That contest ended as a tie and went into sudden-death overtime, when Baltimore got into position on the Giants' 12-yard line. Johnny Unitas went back to pass and threw a ten-yard out to Mutscheller, who caught the ball going out of bounds to set up a first and goal at the two. Then Johnny handed the ball to fullback Alan "the Horse" Ameche, who barreled his way into the end zone for a touchdown and Baltimore won the game. Afterward, a reporter asked Johnny about his pass to Mutscheller: "Why would you throw in a situation like that? What if there had been an interception?"

Johnny said, "When you know what you're doing, you don't throw interceptions."

And guess who coached the Colts in that game? The same guy with rolled-up pants and white shoelaces on his black shoes pacing on the Jets' sideline. Good ole Coach Weeb Ewbank, our leader.

* * *

Man, there's still a lot of clock left, and I can see that I'm itching for my hand to get back to normal so I can get back in—a feeling I can still sense in my house fifty years later. After the Colts go three and out on Johnny's first series, I know I'm not thinking about running the clock out. When you get stung like we did in the Heidi game, that kind of pain has a powerful way of staying with a team. Also, we're only up thirteen and that's not even two touchdowns. Might sound obvious, but it's worth repeating here that there's a big difference between being two scores up, rather than three—especially when playing a team as talented as the '68 Colts. So we still needed to contribute on offense.

We got the ball on our 37-yard line and start off with a Snell run right up the middle. Then I called a deep route for Sauer, but right after getting to the end of my dropback, I saw a blue jersey barreling down on me. Sauer looked like he was open, but that was the formidable Bubba Smith coming at me. When I threw it, I tried to get it to George's outside, but it was a misfire.

No harm, though, because on the next play the Colts brought the house, and I hit Sauer on a hot read for the first down. When he was tackled, though, the ball popped out, and even though the ref marked him down, I keep rewinding the video to see if it was a fumble. Today it would have been automatically reviewed.

It's wonderful to have the ability to do this when watching a game so old. Makes me think about how we perceive and play the game so differently now. Nobody is even questioning the refs here. But if I were a Colt, this play would stick in my craw.

The clock kept running, though, and I wanted to maintain the pressure, so we ran Sixty-go, figuring the Colts would be playing the run. That call gave us maximum protection and only three receivers running routes: Lammons down the middle, Sauer and Maynard on the outside. I was going to go downtown to one of the three. I took a deep drop and looked to George first, and he was open! He had a step or two on corner Lenny Lyles and I threw a strike and we get a good gainer.

Now we were in an excellent position to score. The third quarter came to an end while we continued to play with poise and execution.

CHAPTER FIFTEEN

When I came to Alabama, Coach Bear Bryant had all the freshmen in for a first meeting where he said, "You'll remember the losses quicker than the wins. We're going to win a lot of games, but the losses will stick in y'all's craws."

And that is true to life, man. In the 1970s, I was sitting there in Vegas with my buddy Jimmy, an Irish-Hungarian, in a nice suite with my drink after we'd lost a couple thousand dollars.

I had my beverage and I was telling Jimmy to calm down. He was all worked up and had his shirt off and had these red blotches on his neck and pale sweaty skin. I mean, he was huffing and puffing, reminding me of the redheaded, red-mustached cartoon character Yosemite Sam.

"Hey, cool it, Jimmy. We'll go back downstairs and get it back."

"No!" he says. "No, no, no. I'm not going back down. I quit!"

"What do you mean, you quit? Let's go downstairs and we'll get it back."

"No! I just figured this out."

"Figured what out?"

"Joe! What we win, we don't need anymore. What we lose? It's damn near killing me!"

That made me pause. I said it over again in my head.

What we win, we don't need anymore. What we lose? It's damn near killing me!

He had a point. To this day, it still holds true.

And it comes to mind, when I return to the Super Bowl III game. We were thinking about that next score, nothing more and nothing less. We weren't about to get greedy. From this position on the field, a field goal would put us three scores up on a team that hadn't scored yet. We ran Snell and then Mathis, who both got short gains before we set up for a field goal. Schmitt, our center, made the perfect snap to Parilli. The blocking was good and Turner kicked the ball through the uprights, making the game 16–0.

Now, in an era before two-point conversions, the Colts needed a way to get three scores against the AFL's best defense.

We kicked off and there came Johnny U again. He got his squad to the line, then handed the ball off to Matte for seven yards. It looked like Johnny was maintaining his tradition of firing his team up, and that gain got my attention. During this series, I do remember looking up and seeing six minutes and change and thinking, Please God, let that clock run. In all the games I played, I always said a prayer, but never to ask God for a victory, just to play my best and for everybody to stay injury free. But now, I was asking for some help with the clock.

Then a quick pass to Mackey for five yards, then a Matte run for seven more, and then another completion to Richardson before Matte carried again, this time for another nineteen yards. They need three scores and our defense is softening up in our secondary, to make sure Johnny doesn't pass over their heads for a quick strike. We want them to burn the clock.

The Colts are already in our territory, setting up on our 37. Johnny calls another run and gives the ball to Jerry Hill, who followed his blockers for another twelve yards. After an incompletion to Richardson, the Colts' body language began to show frustration. Johnny called a play with max protection, dropped back, and with no pressure, took a moment to read his options. Looking at the tape, it's clear he made the right decision by going to Jimmy Orr up the seam. But Johnny just doesn't have enough velocity behind the ball, and our cornerback Randy Beverly timed it perfectly, snatching it out of the air in our end zone. Beverly then did the smart thing and took a seat for a touchback after securing the interception, which is the Jets' fourth for the day.

In my kitchen, I watch myself getting the offense together on the field, I'm feeling a bit of sadness for number 19. But in that huddle, in that fourth quarter, on that drive, I was too focused to think about anything but the defense in front of me and what they were giving us.

Now, again, it was all about running the time out. So much so that when the Colts called time-out, Weeb and I looked up at the clock and he asked what I liked.

"I'd like to keep the clock running."

"What do you think of seventy-four-eight?" Weeb said, a pass play.

"You know, Coach, they haven't scored on our defense yet. I'd rather not throw. I'd like to run."

Defensive line coach Buddy Ryan was standing right there, and he gave a nod and hustled over to his defensive guys.

Weeb nodded. "Go ahead."

Johnny might have been okay throwing when he knew what he was doing, but I was fine finishing the Championship Game as the only quarterback to not have thrown a fourth-quarter pass.

In the huddle I was calling plays and also telling everyone to check with me at the line. First it was Boozer for two, then Snell for two, then Boozer again for seven yards. We were milking the clock, taking our time at the line of scrimmage, executing the same plays we've been running the entire game. Again, Baltimore was not going to change for us. Not now.

Then, after a ten-yard gain by Snell on first-and-10, he was pushed out of bounds and a penalty flag flew. Without replay and a distinct memory of what happened, I can't reflect on the play, but I rewind a few times and assume that the personal foul was a late hit. The Colt player is not happy, and I'm just curious at this point, so I click on the sound to confirm, but nothing definitive comes of it.

A little tidbit from the announcer makes me smile, though: "Let's see. They dropped the flag here. There are some hard feelings going on now in this game. Johnny Sample has sort of been the boy that has stirred it up."

Another announcer chimes in: "Of course these hard feelings have been building up down here, you know, for the last ten days as both clubs come into their training camps, statements being printed by one side or the other, saying what's going to happen to the other side—"

Meanwhile, as we were running the clock, our defense was getting their wind back and hydrating, which was not always the case back in the Alabama days. During our first practice

by every team that has ever played football. It's not a given that it's automatic. The ball could slip out of the quarter-back's hands or he could hit an elbow sticking it into the running back's pocket. Even after the running back gets it, there have been cases where he doesn't put it away and flat-out drops the ball. Also, the running back hasn't even been hit by the defense yet, which was going to be doing every-thing possible to knock that pigskin loose.

* * *

When the broadcast picks back up, I see myself jogging onto the field with our guys. I'm happy this tape and so much other material exists about the game, because it allows me to relive so many of the moments, sparking the feelings, emotions, excitement, and adrenaline of being on that field fifty years ago. We were on our own 20-yard line. Two twenty-one left in the game. I got the ball cleanly from our center and executed a good exchange with Matt on the hand-off. On second down I handed off to Matt, who wrapped both arms around the rock to secure it. On third down, we're not looking to fix what isn't broken, so I handed off to Snell again and he gets a *huge* first down for us.

Most of the day we'd been running to our left, but these last three plays we'd run to our right side behind guard Randy Rasmussen, tackle Dave Herman, and tight end Pete Lammons.

I know I've never handed the ball off to a running back, any running back, six times in a row in my life, but that's what we're about to do. Six times in a row! Watching Matt play after play continues to amaze me. I am in awe. I'm think-ing about Matt's endurance, his heart—how can he take all those hits and still run like a teenager? I don't know how he's doing it. Where is he finding the strength? I know Matt would thank his offensive linemen up front doing the dirty work, but his effort and determination were spectacular.

The broadcast keeps flashing to Earl Morrall on the sidelines. Watching it now on a screen, it does not make me feel good about what he's going through. Morrall was MVP of the NFL that year and got pulled. His body posture tells it all. Earl was a class act. A quiet guy who carried himself with a dignity that was rare, throughout the highs and the lows.

I may have never gotten pulled from a big game, but I certainly knew what it was like to be frustrated in one. My third college game was against Vanderbilt. We were ranked number two in the country and favored to win by a big margin. I missed a receiver, and we had to punt. As I came off the field I threw my helmet.

I sat down on the bench, head down, all pissed off, and next thing I knew I felt this big hand around my neck. Coach Bryant had come to the bench and sat down next to me. He put his hand around my neck and started to squeeze.

"Boy, if you ever come off the field like that again, I'll kick your ass all the way back to Beaver Falls."

"Coach, I'm not pissed off at you or any other coach. I'm pissed at myself for playing so bad."

He looked at me and after a few seconds loosened his grip, then got up and left.

I had lost my poise. That was the only time I ever threw my helmet. My helmet didn't even go airborne when I threw five interceptions a couple times as a pro.

But back to the game, or what's left of it. With fifteen seconds remaining, Coach Ewbank sent Curley and the punting team out onto the field. Now, it was critical that we didn't allow the Colts to block the punt. Our center, Paul

Crane, had to snap the ball fifteen yards back on target, and he delivered a strike. Curley used a quick one-step punt technique to get the ball off.

Two plays later, the gun went off. This game was so big that I only allowed myself to believe we'd won once I heard that pistol fire. There was the absolute elation of knowing that for that moment you had reached the top of your sport.

It was over, and I started getting off the field. I walked with Jim Richards, and Hudson came over and gave me a hug as we headed to the locker room. Don Shinnick, one of the Colt's defensive captains, came over and took my arm. He looked me straight in the eyes and said, "Joe, remember God—the Good Lord is with you."

"I do, I always do, Don. Thank you," I replied.

Then we just wanted to get the heck off the field. The security detail dressed in black suits came running out and led us to the locker rooms. The game before, at Shea Stadium, I'd experienced the win that got us to the championship and remembered what it was like when everybody climbed out of the seats and charged onto the field. But this time there was no loitering and shaking hands or exchanging jerseys. We were all off the field as quickly as possible. I still don't even know how Shinnick got over to me so quickly.

As I was jogging toward the tunnel to the locker room, I looked up at all the Jets fans above in the stands, happy faces filled with excitement and joy. They inspired me to put up my hand and wave my finger in a number-one salute. That was all I did to celebrate. I'd never done it before, or since. But that number one that I held up, was as much for the AFL as it was for the Jets and our fans. We had won. The AFL. The Jets. The fans. The underdogs.

CHAPTER SIXTEEN

When we got to the locker room, there was celebrating. All that had been put into getting there and then pulling off a victory was hard to digest in a single moment. It's just the constant awareness of having the opportunity to play in the biggest game of your life. Every next game should be the biggest game, because it's the next one, but to play in the Super Bowl, the World Championship of professional football—well, for *me* there was nothing bigger.

We had done it and won the game and there was joy everywhere. We didn't even care there wasn't champagne in our locker room. The story we heard was that it had been delivered to the Colts' dressing room before the game. I don't know if that's true, and it made no difference to us either way. We'd won.

A reporter asked me if this was a historic win, being that much of an underdog and winning so handily. What a question!

I didn't even want to look at him. It wasn't him personally, but the same guys who had mocked the Jets and the AFL were now shoving mics around changing their tunes.

"I don't know about that," I muttered, looking downward. "I know it's a hell of a loss for those folks who picked it the other way."

That was enough. I wasn't bitter anymore. I wanted to savor the moment so I just turned into my locker and started getting undressed. My dad came over with my brother Bob and Mike Bite. They were happy, of course, and celebrating. Bob came up to me and said, "You did it," and slaps my back.

That was the first time he'd ever congratulated me. It took a while, but hey, I finally did something that impressed my big brother.

I actually ended up going into the training room after they left because the locker room was just too crowded. The training room was out of bounds to everyone but trainers, coaches, players, and owners, and I didn't want to spend much time with the media right then. There was a bit of an attitude, too, in the sense that the media and the oddsmakers had been telling us how badly we were going to get our butts kicked over the past two weeks. This victory, the biggest upset in professional football championship history, was for *all* underdogs to be shared by all the underdogs. Don't ever let people tell you that you can't accomplish something you have a passion for.

I was there in the training room for a while, getting undressed and relaxing on a table, when Sal Marchiano came in with a camera and a couple of guys. Sal had peeked his head around the doorway and I waved him in. I respected him, and he was a local New York sports reporter we all knew. He requested a brief interview.

He asked some questions and then ended by proclaiming, "You're king of the hill!" I laughed, but he continued, saying, "You did it!"

And like I said at the start of this book, "No, no...*we're* king of the hill. We got the team, brother."

I took my time getting showered and dressed and met Joe Hirsch and Suzie Storm, my girlfriend at the time and one of the true loves of my life, outside in the waiting area. We got into Joe's car, which was part of the Jets motorcade.

There was action all around us, but inside the car it was quiet as we waited for the buses and police cars in front of us to get moving. I was thinking, and neither one of them were saying a word. We were driving in a calm peace, and then I just started chuckling. There was no reason, and it wasn't about anything funny. But it was contagious. Some more chuckles, and then Suzie started giggling. Then Joe started. Mine grew into a full release of happiness. There was just so much pressure being released, so much happiness being shared, that words weren't necessary.

I remember driving back to the hotel, laughing from feeling all that joy.

ACKNOWLEDGMENTS

Writing this acknowledgment has been nearly as difficult as writing the book itself. I've mulled over nearly ever mentor, coach, doctor, trainer, and teammate and tried including them in one way or another. Hopefully my gratitude toward them comes through in these pages. Ultimately though, I realized that without three people this book just wouldn't be here.

First and foremost, I've got to thank my best friend and longtime business partner who's been runnin' with me since '61. Without Mr. James C. Walsh, writing a book would never have occurred to me.

Mort, man, you hung in there with me and my Gemini nature. I needed your patience and appreciated you reminding me that this was my book.

And perhaps as only a daughter can, Jessica Grace, you reminded me of different stories and the color I might've told them with over the years. You certainly helped me open up about things and made sure that everything was written as I'd say it.

Finally, to all my teammates in life who gave such unselfish, relentless effort from my backyard to Super Bowl III...we did it.

ABOUT THE AUTHOR

Joe Namath has been a reluctant author since he was able to write. Choosing sports over schoolwork unless absolutely necessary, he was a quarterback for the University of Alabama, where he won a National Championship. He went on to be drafted to the New York Jets where he was AFL Rookie of the Year, twice AFL Most Valuable Player, NFL passing touchdowns leader, NFL passing yards leader, NFL Comeback Player of the Year, a George S. Halas Courage Award winner, the MVP of Super Bowl III, and a member of the Pro Football Hall of Fame. His dashing good looks led him into the enterprising arms of Hollywood, where he performed on screen and stage, legitimizing his "Broadway Joe" nickname in *The Caine Mutiny Court Martial*. Despite all the years of practice, however, Namath still struggles with writing even the simplest thank-you note because of his insatiable urge to get outside and play.